A Game Plan for Effective Leadership: Lessons from 10 Successful Coaches in Moving Theory to Practice
From Leadership Theory to Practice: A Game Plan for Success as a Leader
Practical Leadership Strategies: Lessons from the World of Professional Baseball
Going Back to the Future: A Leadership Journey for Educators
A Path to Leadership: The Heroic Follower
Leadership with a Conscience: Educational Leadership as a Moral Science
Educational Administration: Leading with Mind and Heart, 3rd Edition
Law and American Education: A Case Brief Approach, 3rd Edition
A Commonsense Approach to Educational Leadership
No Laughing Matter: The Value of Humor in Educational Leadership
Feminist Theory and Educational Leadership: Much Ado about Something!

A TEN-MINUTE APPROACH TO EDUCATIONAL LEADERSHIP

A Handbook of Insights for All Level Administrators

Robert Palestini

ROWMAN & LITTLEFIELD EDUCATION

A division of
ROWMAN & LITTLEFIELD PUBLISHERS, INC.
Lanham • New York • Toronto • Plymouth, UK

Published by Rowman & Littlefield Education
A division of Rowman & Littlefield Publishers, Inc.
A wholly owned subsidiary of The Rowman & Littlefield Publishing Group, Inc.
4501 Forbes Boulevard, Suite 200, Lanham, Maryland 20706
www.rowman.com

10 Thornbury Road, Plymouth PL6 7PP, United Kingdom

Copyright © 2013 by Robert Palestini

All rights reserved. No part of this book may be reproduced in any form or by any electronic or mechanical means, including information storage and retrieval systems, without written permission from the publisher, except by a reviewer who may quote passages in a review.

British Library Cataloguing in Publication Information Available

Library of Congress Cataloging-in-Publication Data

Palestini, Robert H.
  A ten-minute approach to educational leadership : a handbook of insights for all level administrators / Robert Palestini.
      pages cm
  Includes bibliographical references.
  ISBN 978-1-4758-0304-4 (cloth : alk. paper) — ISBN 978-1-4758-0305-1 (pbk. : alk. paper) — ISBN 978-1-4758-0306-8 (electronic) 1. School management and organization. I. Title.
  LB2801.A1P35 2013
  371.2--dc23
                                                              2013018810

To Tom Koerner, whose longtime faith in me
as an author is much appreciated.

To Carlie Wall, for her invaluable contributions.

To Judy, whose support and encouragement mean the world to me.

To Karen, Scott, Rob, and Brendan,
whose presence in my life is rejuvenating.

To Rob, for his creativity in drawing the figures for this book.

To Liz and Wendy, for willingly providing
much-needed technical assistance.

CONTENTS

INTRODUCTION ix

1 **ONE-MINUTE ASSESSMENT OF THE ORGANIZATIONAL STRUCTURE** 1

2 **ONE-MINUTE ASSESSMENT OF THE ORGANIZATIONAL CULTURE** 7

3 **ONE-MINUTE ASSESSMENT OF THE LEADERSHIP BEHAVIOR** 17

4 **ONE-MINUTE ASSESSMENT OF THE MOTIVATIONAL PROCESS** 31

5 **ONE-MINUTE ASSESSMENT OF THE COMMUNICATION PROCESS** 41

6 **ONE-MINUTE ASSESSMENT OF THE DECISION-MAKING PROCESS** 51

7 **ONE-MINUTE ASSESSMENT OF THE CONFLICT MANAGEMENT PROCESS** 63

CONTENTS

8	**ONE-MINUTE ASSESSMENT OF THE DISTRIBUTION OF POWER**	69
9	**ONE-MINUTE ASSESSMENT OF THE STRATEGIC PLANNING PROCESS**	83
10	**ONE-MINUTE ASSESSMENT OF THE TOLERANCE FOR CHANGE**	91
11	**ONE-MINUTE ASSESSMENT OF LEADING WITH HEART**	105
12	**WHAT HAVE WE LEARNED?**	119
	APPENDIX: HEART SMART SURVEYS I AND II	125
	REFERENCES	139
	ABOUT THE AUTHOR	143

INTRODUCTION

How often have we visited or heard about educational institutions where there were "strong" administrators whose institutions seemed to win while the people in them lost? Some of their supervisors thought that they were effective administrators, while many of their coworkers and subordinates thought otherwise. Many of these administrators would depict themselves as no-nonsense managers who "kept on top of the situation and had everything under control." We have heard pride in their voices as they proclaim their credo that "Nice guys (and gals) finish last."

On the other hand, many of us have observed and met many "nice guy" (and gal) administrators whose people seemed to win while their institutions lost. Some of the people who reported to them thought they were effective administrators, but those to whom they reported had their doubts. These administrators would claim that they were "collaborative," "participative," and even "humanistic." We heard pride in their voices as they declared themselves "people persons."

It is as though most administrators in the world are primarily interested either in results or people, but not necessarily both. Really effective administrators, however, manage themselves and the people they work with so that both their institutions and the people benefit from their presence.

INTRODUCTION

In their extremely engaging and enlightening book, *The One Minute Manager*, Kenneth Blanchard and Spencer Johnson express in allegorical terms the three "secrets" to being an effective manager. Their three secrets are:

1. One-minute goal setting
2. One-minute praising
3. One-minute reprimanding

Blanchard and Johnson suggest that taking one minute each day to consider each of these three secrets will result in effective management. Accepting these points as a good beginning, I suggest that we supplement them with ten "secrets" of my own.

Just as many individuals in their spiritual lives periodically examine their consciences by filtering their moral and ethical behavior through the lens of the Ten Commandments or some comparable moral code, I am suggesting that educational leaders take ten minutes each day to filter their leadership behavior through the lens of the "Ten Commandments" of organizational development listed below. I would also include an "Eleventh Commandment," which I call leading with heart. Thus, I would suggest spending just one minute every day pondering each of the following components of a healthy and successful organization:

1. One-minute assessment of the organizational *structure*
2. One-minute assessment of the organizational *culture*
3. One-minute assessment of the organizational *leadership*
4. One-minute assessment of the *motivational process*
5. One-minute assessment of the *communication process*
6. One-minute assessment of the *decision-making process*
7. One-minute assessment of the *conflict management process*
8. One-minute assessment of the *empowerment process*
9. One-minute assessment of the *strategic planning process*
10. One-minute assessment of the *change process*

The above components of an organization like a school, school system, or university speak to the so-called science of leadership but do not neces-

INTRODUCTION

sarily relate to the art of administration and leadership. And one needs to lead with both mind (science) and heart (art) to be truly effective. So the effective building blocks of quality leadership are the skills of communication, motivation, organizational development, management, and creativity. Mastering the theory and practice in these areas of study will produce high-quality leadership ability and, in turn, produce successful leaders; doing so with "heart" or compassion will result in not only highly successful leadership, but what author and scholar Chris Lowney calls "heroic leadership." Figure I.1 depicts the ten assessments that, when applied in an integrated fashion and with heart, complete the jigsaw puzzle of effective educational administration.

So picture yourself standing in the middle of a dense forest. Suppose you were asked to describe the characteristics of the forest. What types of

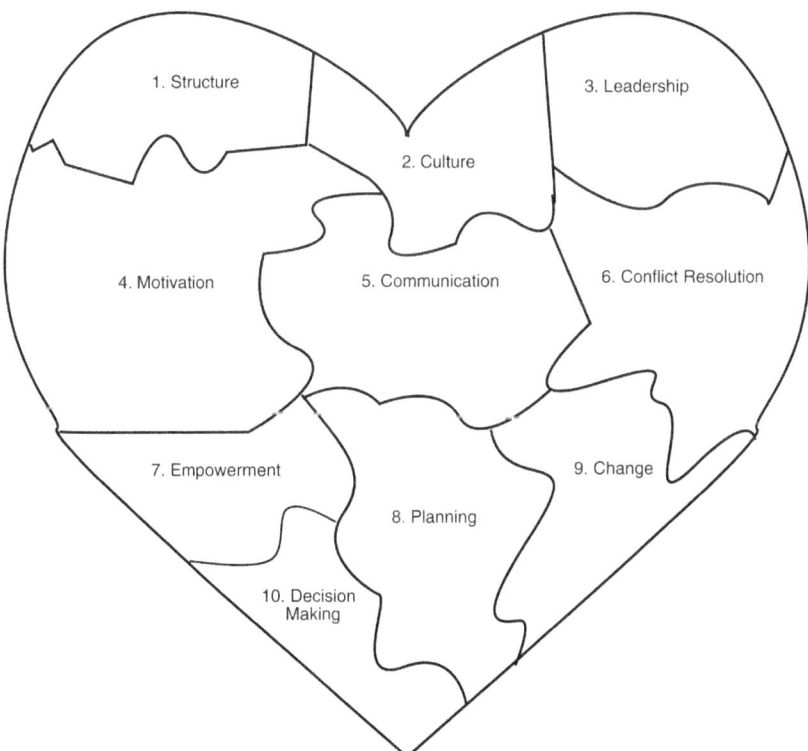

Figure I.1.   Jigsaw Puzzle of Effective Leadership

trees are growing? Where are the trees thriving? Where are they not? Faced with this proposition, most people would not be able to see the forest for the trees.

Newly appointed and not so newly appointed administrators often have these same feelings of confusion when faced with the prospect of assuming a leadership role in a complex organization like a school, a school system, or a college. Where does one start? An effective way to start would be to systematically examine the components that comprise an organization. Such a process of organizational diagnosis and prescription will lead to a comprehensive and integrated analysis of the organization's strengths and weaknesses and point the way toward improvement. This book suggests such a sequential and systematic approach. Utilizing it effectively can produce dramatic results.

Each chapter of this book is dedicated to one of the ten essential components of an organization like a school, school system, or university. Most of each chapter focuses on the implementation of these components, but there is some emphasis on the supporting theory that speaks to *why* these leadership practices are effective. We know that administrators are busy people; therefore, at the end of each chapter is a diagnostic checklist of questions that should be helpful in *quickly* assessing the status of these components in your institution and whether they need to be addressed. In the appendix, there are two diagnostic instruments, Heart Smart Surveys I and II, that will help you quantify the assessment process. If the reader is interested in a more detailed explanation of the concepts covered in this book, I would suggest an earlier publication of mine, *Educational Administration: Leading with Mind and Heart*, third edition (2011). Hopefully, addressing these questions in a systematic and concrete way will enable us to see *both* the forest and the trees and lead our institutions to new heights (pun intended).

1

ONE-MINUTE ASSESSMENT OF THE ORGANIZATIONAL STRUCTURE

The master in the art of living makes little distinction between his work and his play, his labor and his leisure, his mind and his body, his education and his recreation, his love and his religion. He hardly knows which is which. He simply pursues his vision of excellence in whatever he does, leaving others to decide whether he is working or playing. To him, he is always doing both.

—Zen Buddhist text

Educational entities are essentially organized according to one of three basic structures, the classical structure, the social systems structure, or the open systems structure. Despite being organized around one of these structures, most schools and school systems reflect certain aspects of each of these models (De Pree 1989). These structures are illustrated in figure 1.1.

THE CLASSICAL THEORY

Classical theorists believe that an application of a bureaucratic structure and process will promote rational, efficient, and disciplined behavior, making possible the achievement of well-defined goals. Efficiency, then, is achieved

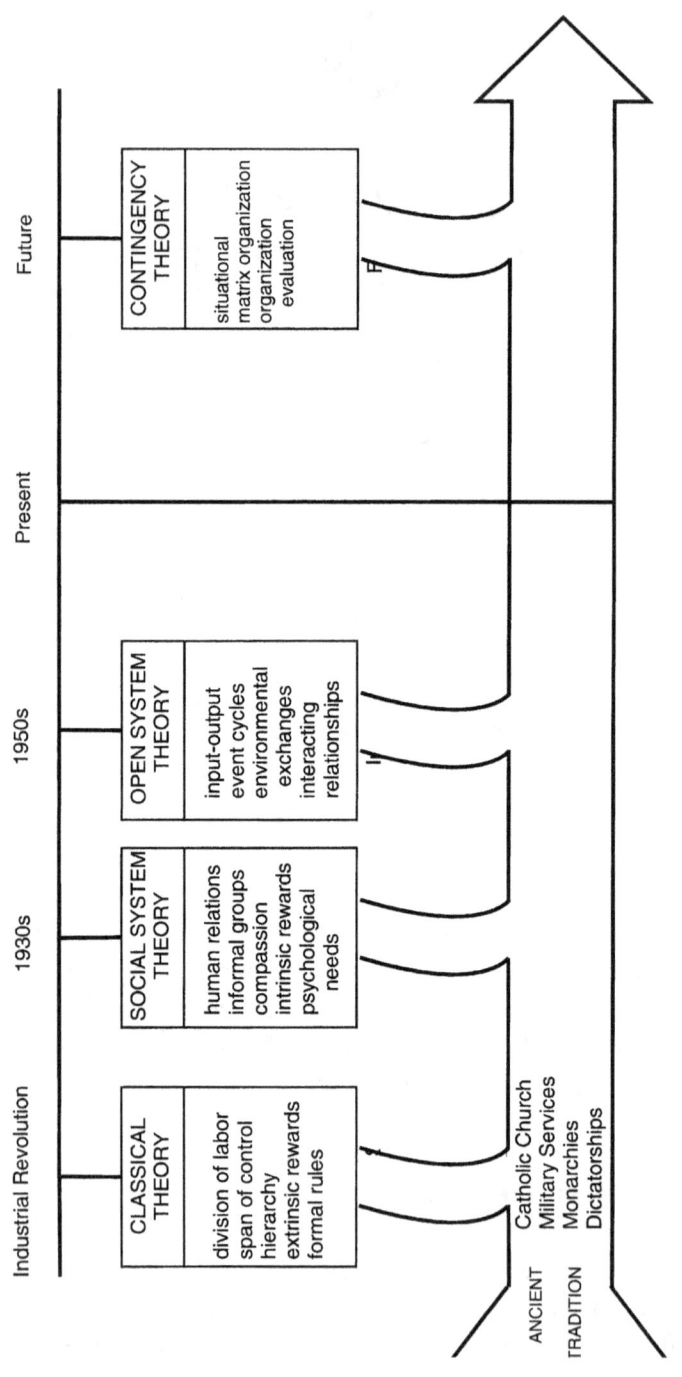

Figure 1.1. Theories of Organizational Structure

by arranging positions and jurisdiction and by placing power at the top of a clear chain of command. The conceptual model of the classical theory has had a significant impact on education. Virtually every school and school system in the United States is organized according to the tenets of the classical theory.

Within the classical theory framework, the individual is conceived of as an object, a part of the bureaucratic machine. This is the antithesis of the second organizational theory, the social systems theory. Historically, researchers found that the impact of social-psychological variables within the worker group was significant. The study of behavior in social system settings intensified, and a greater sophistication developed about how and why group members behave as they do under given conditions. In time a natural social systems orientation to the analysis of behavior evolved in the literature as an alternative to the rational or classical systems approach.

THE SOCIAL THEORY

The conceptual perspective of the social systems model suggests that an organization consists of a collection of groups (social systems) that collaborate to achieve system goals. Coalitions among subgroups within the organization (e.g., English teachers, history teachers, and foreign language teachers) form to provide power bases upon which positive or negative action can be taken (e.g., "Let's all vote to reject writing behavioral objectives."). As with the classical organizational theory, schools and school systems have been profoundly influenced by the social systems model.

THE OPEN SYSTEM THEORY

A newer theory that is having a growing influence on educational institutions, especially higher education institutions, is the open system model. The classical and social system theories tend to view organizational life as a closed system, that is, as isolated from the surrounding environment. In contrast, open system theory conceives of an organization as a set of interrelated parts that interact with the internal and external environments. It receives "inputs" such as human and material resources, values, community expectations, and societal demands; it transforms them through a production process (e.g., an educational program); and it exports the product in the form of "outputs" (e.g., graduates, new knowledge, revised value sets) into the environment (e.g., businesses, the military, service providers, etc.) with "value added." The organization receives a return (e.g., community financial support in the form of taxes or tuition) for its efforts so it can survive and prosper. Then the cycle begins once again. Figure 1.2 illustrates the open system dynamic.

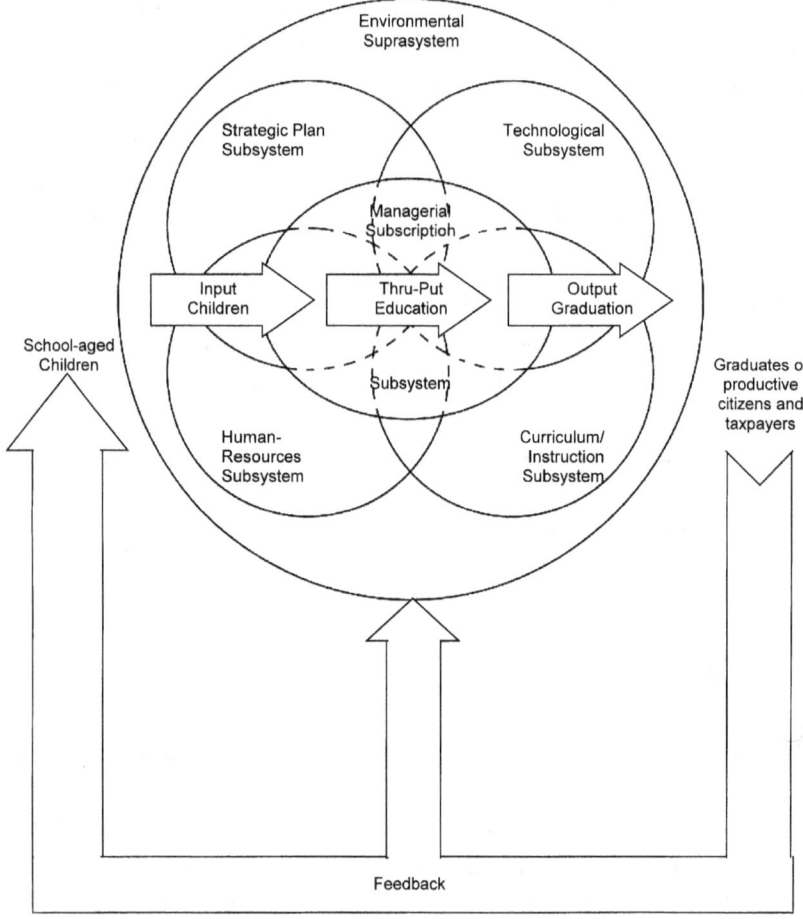

Figure 1.2. Open Systems Dynamics

Through the perspective of open system theory, a new logic on issues of organizational governance has emerged. It emphasizes the relationship of the organization to its surrounding environment and, thus, places a premium on planning and programming for events that cannot be controlled directly. The key to making an open system work effectively and efficiently is its ability to gather, process, and utilize information. In an educational institution, then, the facility with which a need is discovered, a goal is established, and resources are coalesced to meet that need will determine the effectiveness and efficiency of that institution. Unlike businesses, educational institutions, especially colleges and universities, have not yet found a way to meet the demands of the open system model.

CONTINGENCY THEORY

In recent years, a view of organization development has surfaced that treats each organization, and even the entities within the organization, as relatively unique. For centuries, this orientation has been at the core of practitioner behavior, but has been seen basically as an anomaly, reflective of inefficiency or unpreparedness, and thus overlooked by management scientists. Currently, the changing situational character of management is coming to be understood as a key to the management process itself.

Many management scholars and practitioners would now agree with the observation that contingency theory is perhaps the most powerful current and future trend in the organization field. At this stage of development, however, contingency theory is not really a theory. Rather, it is a conceptual tool that facilitates our understanding of the situational flow of events and alternate organizational and individual responses to that flow. Thus, as a conceptual tool, contingency theory does not possess the holistic character of the three major models discussed earlier. In many ways, contingency theory can be thought of as a subset of open system theory because it is through open system theory that we come to understand the dynamic flows of events, personnel, and resources that take place in organizations.

At any rate, the implication of contingency theory is that in order to have a maximally effective organization structure, institutions should employ the best of all three theoretical models—classical, social, and open systems—depending on the situation. Thus, a contingency organizational structure can be described as an institutional mind-set rather than an organizational chart, since, unlike the classical theory, it is difficult to depict the attributes of social and open systems theory in the form of a chart. As a preview of coming attractions, so to speak, we will incorporate contingency theory thinking in our discussion of leadership, employee motivation, communication, decision making, conflict resolution, and virtually all of the ten components of an organization that we cover in this book.

DIAGNOSTIC CHECKLIST

Here are some questions that can be addressed in assessing your institution's organizational structure:

- Are the best aspects of the classical, social systems, and open systems organizational structures present?
- Is there appropriate division of labor, and is it flexible?
- Is the division of labor conducive to reaching organizational goals?
- Is the structure of the organization well designed?
- Is there a respect for human dignity in the organization?
- Do work groups operate effectively and in tandem?
- Does the organization's structure respond to the environmental contingencies?

ONE-MINUTE ASSESSMENT OF THE ORGANIZATIONAL CULTURE

Culture consists of the unwritten laws impressed on the souls of those living under the same constitution.

—*Philo*

The educational leader should take one minute each day to assess the current state of the institution's organizational culture. Every salesperson is advised to get to "know the territory." The astute administrator will take a page from *The Music Man*'s Professor Harold Hill and get to know the territory in his or her educational institution. Knowing the territory in education translates into being keenly aware of the organizational structure and culture of the institution.

Knowing how one's educational entity is structured within the context of the three models described in chapter 1 is the first step in an educational leader's quest to truly "know the territory." The second step is to be aware of the organizational behavior or culture of the institution. Organizational culture is composed of the shared beliefs, expectations, values, and norms of conduct of its members. In any organization, the informal culture interacts with the formal structure and control system to produce a generally clear understanding of the "way things are done around here." Even more than the forces of bureaucracy, the organization's culture is the glue that binds people together.

Anyone who has visited a number of educational institutions develops a sense of their different "personalities" or culture. Walking the hallways and campus of an educational institution, an astute observer can see physical manifestations of an underlying set of values; perhaps a huge trophy case in the entrance lobby, classroom desks bolted to the floor, a clean and attractive campus, football and band programs that overshadow math and science programs, faculty and staff constantly patrolling the halls, clandestine meetings of students or faculty, and so forth. Thus, institutions have been alternately characterized as union schools, football factories, diploma mills, Blue Ribbon schools, schools of excellence, and learning organizations.

The above are tangible aspects of the school's culture. The intangible aspects often parallel those values. Schools attempting to develop shared values and enculturate them are often illustrated by symbols common around the campus: "Knowledge Is Power"; "Wildcat Pride"; "Education Is about Alternatives"; "Just Say No"; and "All Children Achieving." Other symbols of the school's culture are the heroes and storytellers, faculty members and/or administrators who have earned legendary status.

Administrators can influence the institution's culture in a positive way. First, however, they must be aware of its importance and its components. If the educational leader has a thorough knowledge of the institution's culture, he or she can set about trying to influence it. One way of doing so is to take time each day to review this and the nine other "secrets" to effective school management that are presented in this book. Ultimately, the best way to influence the institution's culture is by modeling desired behavior. If the leaders want the faculty and staff to be efficient and effective, the leaders need to manifest those same characteristics in their own behavior. However, none of these desired changes will occur unless a culture of mutual trust and respect has been established.

THE PROCESSES OF ORGANIZATIONAL CULTURE

We now explore areas of organizational culture that deal with the way we perceive events or other people, the way we understand the events and people we perceive, the way our past experiences and acquisition of knowledge and information influence this description and diagnosis, and the way we form attitudes about the situations based on our perceptions, understanding, and experience. These four processes are referred to as perception, attribution, learning, and attitude formation. Understanding them greatly enhances an administrator's ability to influence the school's culture.

Perception

Perception is the process by which each person senses reality and comes to a particular understanding or view. It is an active process that results in different people having somewhat different, even contradictory, views or understandings of the same event or person. Rarely do different observers describe events or persons in exactly the same way. Often, administrators and their subordinates, coworkers, or supervisors see and describe the same situation differently.

Perceptual Distortion

Perceptions sometimes suffer from inaccuracies or distortions. Although such biases are normal and human, they can have significant consequences when administrators or other members of the institution base action upon potentially invalid distortions. We discuss stereotyping, the halo effect, projection, and the self-fulfilling prophecy as examples. Additional distortions include suppression, repression, denial, displacement, and rationalization (Brodsky 1988).

Stereotyping. Stereotyping occurs when an individual attributes behaviors or attitudes to a person on the basis of the group or category to which that person belongs. "Women teachers can't control a class" and "Principals are all dictators" illustrate stereotyping. We frequently stereotype people on the basis of their ethnicity or gender, or of their role, such as administrator, faculty member, or support personnel.

Why does stereotyping occur? Often individuals do not gather sufficient data about others to describe their behaviors or attitudes accurately. They may look for shortcuts to describe certain phenomena without spending the time to analyze them completely. Alternatively, some individuals have personal biases against certain groups of individuals. Historical attitudes toward certain cultural groups may result in stereotypes. Americans may have certain views of Europeans and different views of Japanese, based on their historical experiences with the two groups. Using stereotypes reduces the accuracy of our perceptions about these groups.

The Halo Effect. The halo effect refers to an individual letting one salient feature of a person dominate the evaluation of that individual. A willingness to volunteer for extra projects, for example, can cause an administrator to evaluate a teacher as highly competent in the classroom. A neat personal appearance can cause a person to be judged as precise in his or her work and very well organized.

The halo effect frequently occurs in assessments of teacher performance. Individuals may be judged on the basis of one trait, for example, promptness, neatness, or enthusiasm, rather than on a composite of traits and skills over a period of time (Heilman and Stopeck 1985).

Projection. Have you ever heard a teacher say, "my principal is prejudiced," "my supervisor doesn't like women," or "my superintendent doesn't like minorities"? These observations about these administrators may be accurate, but they may also be a reflection of the teachers' prejudices. Or consider the principal who hesitantly approaches a prospective student's parent, feeling that the parent will not think that the school will offer a quality education to the child. The principal may be seeing his or her own attitudes or feelings about the school in the parent's response, whether or not the parent really feels that way.

Projection refers to an individual's attribution of his or her own attitudes or feelings to another person. Individuals use projection as a defense mechanism, to transfer blame to another person, or to provide protection from their own unacceptable feelings. Individuals frequently attribute their own prejudices against minorities, supervisors, or employees. Hence, projection and its dysfunctional consequences can increase as the workforce becomes more diverse; individuals who lack understanding or mistrust people who are different from themselves may project these insecurities onto others.

Self-fulfilling Prophecy. In many situations, individuals expect certain behaviors from other individuals or groups. They then see these behaviors as occurring, whether or not they actually do. Their expectations become self-fulfilling prophecies. They may expect workers to be lazy, bossy, or tardy; then they perceive them as lazy, bossy, or tardy. These expectations may be associated with stereotyping, the halo effect, or projection.

Our expectations influence our perceptions of others, reducing their accuracy; they also have been shown to influence the performance of those of whom we have expectations. We are all familiar with the many studies that have linked teacher expectations and student achievement. If a teacher expects a minority student to fail, oftentimes the student does fail. If a teacher expects all children to achieve, however, the children usually achieve. Likewise, if teachers think that their school is going to close as part of a district reorganization plan, the self-fulfilling prophecy often takes effect and teachers' morale and performance decline, and as a result the school actually does close.

Dealing with Distortions

How can we reduce dysfunctional perceptual distortions in organizations? First, individuals must gather sufficient information about other people's behavior and attitudes to encourage more realistic perceptions. Administrators, for example, must judge an individual's performance on his or her observed behavior, rather than on the behavior of a group to which the person belongs. Second, administrators must check the conclusions they draw to ensure their validity. Third, they must differentiate between facts and assumptions in determining the basis of their perceptions. Fourth, they must distinguish among various aspects of an individual's behavior, rather than grouping even superficially related aspects. They must separate appearance from performance, productivity from attendance, personality from creativity. Fifth, to eliminate or reduce projection, individuals must first identify their true feelings. Do they feel anger, uncertainty, and mistrust? After recognizing these feelings, administrators must repeatedly assess whether and how they are influencing their perceptions of others.

The Attribution Process

The need to determine why events occur is inherent in the diagnostic approach that good administrators often take toward problem solving. Many of us, whether consciously or not, first ponder the reasons for an event and then decide why the event occurred. In this way, we attribute causes to the events. We move from description to diagnosis. As might be expected, different people often attribute different causes to the same event.

Attribution theorists and researchers have studied the process of determining the causes of specific events, the responsibility for particular outcomes, and the personal qualities of individuals participating in the situation. We might consider, for example, that the introduction of a new curriculum was the major explanation for a decline in a teacher's performance; if so, we will attribute the decline to situational factors. If, on the other hand, we feel that laziness or ineptitude influenced performance, then we are likely to conclude that personal dispositions caused the change. Although both situational and personal factors may have influenced the change in performance, we often simplify our understanding and attend primarily to only one cause.

Attribution and Locus of Control

Attribution and the concept of locus of control are closely related. Locus of control is the feeling an individual has about whether he or she is in control of his or her own destiny. Whether one believes that internal or external factors affect future events determines whether one has an internal or external locus of control. Those with an internal locus of control believe that future events are determined by their own individual abilities and personal qualities, while those with an external locus of control attribute future outcomes to factors outside of their control.

Thus, the student who attributes a poor performance on a test to the teacher's inability to get the subject across can be said to have an external locus of control, while the student who attributes the poor performance to his or her own lack of preparation would tend to have an internal locus of control. The objective, then, for school administrators would be to develop a strong internal locus of control in both themselves and their staffs (Kelley 1967).

The Learning Process

In addition to perception and attribution, learning, which refers to the acquisition of skills, knowledge, ability, or attitudes, influences the organizational culture of an educational institution. In this section, we focus on the way individuals learn, beginning with three models of learning and concluding with the administrative implications of learning.

The Behaviorist Approach

Behaviorists emphasize external influences and the power of rewards in learning. They emphasize the link between a given stimulus and response. Recall Pavlov's groundbreaking work with dogs. He noted that, upon presentation of powdered meat blown through a tube (unconditioned stimulus) to a dog, the dog salivated (unconditioned response). The ringing of a bell (neutral stimulus) yielded no salivation responses. After pairing the ringing bell with the meat several times, Pavlov then rang the bell without the meat, and the dog salivated (conditioned response). In classical conditioning, after repeated pairing of neutral and unconditioned stimuli, solitary presentation of the neutral stimulus led to a conditioned response (Pavlov 1927).

Operant conditioning extends classical conditioning to focus on the consequences of a behavior. While a stimulus can still cue a response behavior, the desired or undesired consequence that follows the behavior determines whether the behavior will recur. For example, an individual who receives a bonus (a positive consequence) after creative performance (behavior) on a work assignment (stimulus) is more likely to repeat the creative behavior than if his or her performance is ignored (a negative consequence).

The Cognitive Approach

In contrast to the behavior-reinforcement links that are central to behaviorist theories, cognitive theorists emphasize the internal mental processes involved in gaining new insights. They view learning as occurring from the joining of various cues in the environment into a mental map. In early cognitive experiments, rats learned to run through a maze to reach a goal of food. Repeated trials would cause a rat to develop and strengthen cognitive connections that identified the correct path to the goal (Tolman 1932).

Employees, too, can develop a cognitive map that shows the path to a specific goal. In this case, the cognitive processes join the stimulus to result in a given behavior. On-the-job training, like a new teacher induction process, should result in a new cognitive map of job performance for junior teachers.

The Social Learning Approach

Extending beyond both behavioral and cognitive learning theories, social learning theory integrates the behaviorist and cognitive approaches with the idea of modeling or imitating behaviors. Learners first watch others who act as models, next develop a mental picture of the behavior and its consequences, and finally try the behavior. If positive consequences result, the learner repeats the behavior; if negative consequences occur, no repetition occurs.

The learning impact occurs when the subject tries the behavior and experiences a favorable result, as in the behaviorist approach. At the same time, the learner's development of a cognitive image of the situation incorporates a basic aspect of cognitive learning. The existence of social learning makes it important that teachers take their responsibility of acting as exemplars for the students very seriously. In addition, administrators need to model the behavior that they expect of the faculty (Bandura 1978).

MANAGERIAL IMPLICATIONS OF LEARNING

How can school administrators encourage their own and others' learning in the workplace? They can ensure that appropriate conditions for learning exist; providing appropriate stimuli (e.g., professional development materials) should facilitate acquisition of the skills or attitudes desired. Administrators should reinforce desired learned behaviors. They should also provide environmental cues that encourage learning; structuring a context that supports learning is essential. In effect, just as we advise teachers to adapt their teaching styles to the variety of learning styles of their students, administrators must adapt their management styles to the variety of learning styles that are present among their faculties.

Administrators can use the following modeling strategy, for example. First, the administrator should identify the goal or target behaviors that will lead to improved performance. For example, a more extensive use of cooperative learning activities will lead to improving students' social skills. Second, the administrator must select the appropriate model and determine whether to present the model through a live demonstration, video, other media, or a combination of all of these. Third, the administrator must be sure the teachers are capable of meeting the technical skill requirements of the target behavior. For example, further training might be necessary. Fourth, the administrator must structure a favorable and positive learning environment to increase the likelihood that the teachers will learn the new behavior and act in the desired way. Starting cooperative learning with a particularly skilled teacher and a cooperative group of students will ensure success. Fifth, administrators must model the target behavior and carry out supporting activities, such as role playing. Conducting a faculty meeting using cooperative learning techniques would be an example of such a strategy. Sixth, they should positively reinforce reproduction of the target behaviors both in training and in the workplace. Teacher-of-the-month awards are an example of this strategy. Once the target behaviors are reproduced, administrators must maintain and strengthen them through a system of rewards until the behavior is institutionalized; that is, it becomes part of the school culture. In a nutshell, then, administrators need to model desired behavior and then reward it when it occurs. As a result, our educational institutions will become what Peter Senge refers to as "learning organizations" (Senge 1990).

DEVELOPING POSITIVE ATTITUDES

Another aspect of organizational behavior and culture is attitude formation. An attitude is a consistent predisposition to respond to various aspects of people, situations, or objects that we infer from a person's behavior or expressed attitude, as well as from other cognitive, affective, or connotative responses. Attitudes are pervasive and predict behavior toward their objects. We might, for example, determine an individual's job satisfaction by inferring it from his or her general demeanor on the job or by asking the person to describe this attitude. We often use attitude surveys or other collections of attitude scales to assess individuals' attitudes toward their job, coworkers, supervisor, or the school or school system at large (Greenwald 1989). Once again, being the change one desires in others will go a long way in developing an overall positive attitude in an educational institution.

DIAGNOSTIC CHECKLIST

Here are some questions that can be addressed in assessing your institution's organizational culture:

- Does the organization exhibit a culture of mutual trust and respect?
- Do perceptual distortions proliferate?
- Does the workforce exhibit an internal locus of control?
- Is the institution a learning organization?
- Are the various learning styles being addressed in the management process?
- Is the leader adapting his or her leadership style to the learning style of the followers?
- What beliefs and values do the individuals in the organization have?
- How do these beliefs and values influence individual attitudes?
- What functional and dysfunctional behaviors result from the individuals' perceptions, attributions, learning, and attitudes?
- Are the leaders modeling desired behavior?

ONE-MINUTE ASSESSMENT OF THE LEADERSHIP BEHAVIOR

> *The effective functioning of social systems from the local PTA to the United States of America is assumed to be dependent on the quality of their leadership.*
>
> —*Victor H. Vroom*

Leadership is offered as a solution for most of the problems of organizations everywhere. Schools will work, we are told, if principals provide strong instructional leadership. Universities will be successful if they have visionary leaders. Around the world, administrators and managers say that their organizations would thrive if only senior management provided strategy, vision, and real leadership. Though the call for leadership is universal, there is much less clarity about what the term means (Kirkpatrick and Locke 1991).

Historically, researchers in this field have searched for the one leadership style that would be most effective in all cases. Current thought, however, is that there is no one best style. Rather, a combination of styles depending on the situation in which the leader finds him- or herself has been found to be more appropriate. To understand the evolution of leadership theory thought, we will take a historical approach and trace the progress of leadership theory, beginning with the trait perspective of leadership and moving to the more current contingency theories of leadership.

Trait theory suggests that we can evaluate leadership and propose ways of leading effectively by considering whether an individual possesses certain personality traits, social traits, and physical characteristics. Popular in the 1940s and '50s, trait theory attempted to predict which individuals successfully became leaders and then whether they were effective. Leaders differ from nonleaders in their drive, desire to lead, honesty and integrity, self-confidence, cognitive ability, and knowledge of their fields.

Limitations in the ability of traits to predict effective leadership caused researchers during the 1950s to consider a person's *behavior* rather than that individual's personal traits as a way of increasing leadership effectiveness. This view also paved the way for later behavioral and situational theories.

The types of leadership behaviors investigated typically fell into two categories: production oriented and employee oriented. Production-oriented leadership, also called concern for production, initiating structure, or task-focused leadership, involves acting primarily to get the task done. An administrator who tells his or her science department chair to "do everything he or she needs to do to get the new ecology curriculum developed on time for the start of school, regardless of the personal consequences" demonstrates production-oriented leadership. So does an administrator who uses an autocratic style or fails to involve workers in any aspect of decision making. Employee-oriented leadership, also called concern for people or collaborative leadership, focuses on supporting the individual workers in their activities and involving the workers in decision making. A principal who demonstrates great concern for his or her teachers' job satisfaction and is sensitive to both their personal and professional needs has an employee-oriented leadership style.

SITUATIONAL LEADERSHIP THEORY

Contingency or situational models differ from the earlier trait and behavioral models in asserting that no single way of leading works in all situations. Rather, appropriate behavior depends on the circumstances at a given time. Effective managers diagnose the situation, identify the leadership style that will be most effective, and then determine whether they can implement the required style.

Research suggests that the effect of leader behaviors on performance is altered by such intervening variables as the effort of subordinates, their ability to perform their jobs, the clarity of their job responsibilities, the organization of the work, the cooperation and cohesiveness of the group, the sufficiency of resources and support provided to the group, and the coordination of work group activities with those of other subunits. Thus, leaders must respond to these and broader cultural differences in choosing an appropriate style.

The Bolman/Deal Model

Bolman and Deal have developed a unique situational leadership theory that analyzes leadership behavior through four frames of reference—structural, human resource, political, and symbolic. Each of the frames offers a different perspective on what leadership is and how it operates in organizations. Each can result in either effective or ineffective conceptions of leadership (Bolman and Deal 1991).

Structural leaders develop a new model of the relationship of structure, strategy, and environment for their organizations. They focus on implementation. The right answer helps only if it can be implemented. They are often referred to by their followers as direct, no-nonsense, and hands-on managers. Structural leaders sometimes fail because they miscalculate the difficulty of putting their design in place. They often underestimate the resistance that it will generate, and they take few steps to build a base of support for their innovations. In short, they are often undone by human resource, political, and symbolic considerations. Structural leaders do continually experiment, evaluate, and adapt, but because they fail to consider the entire environment in which they are situated, they sometimes are ineffective.

Human resource leaders believe in people and communicate that belief. They are passionate about "productivity through people." They demonstrate this faith in their words and actions and often build it into a philosophy or credo that is central to their vision of their organizations. Human resource leaders are visible and accessible. Peters and Waterman (1988) popularized the notion of "management wandering around," the idea that managers need to get out of their offices and interact with workers and customers. Many educational administrators have adopted this management principle.

Effective human resource leaders empower; that is, they increase participation, provide support, share information, and move decision making as far down the organization as possible. Human resource leaders often like to refer to their employees as "partners" or "colleagues." They want to make it clear that employees have a stake in the organization's success and a right to be involved in making decisions. When they are ineffective, however, they are seen as naive or as weaklings and wimps.

Political leaders clarify what they want and what they can get. Political leaders are realists above all. They never let what they want cloud their judgment about what is possible. They assess the distribution of power and interests. The political leader needs to think carefully about the players, their interests, and their power; in other words, he or she must map the political terrain. Political leaders ask questions such as, Whose support do I need? How do I go about getting it? Who are my opponents? How much power do they have? What can I do to reduce the opposition? Is the battle winnable? However, if ineffective, these leaders are perceived as being untrustworthy and manipulative.

The symbolic frame provides still a fourth turn of the kaleidoscope of leadership. In this frame, the organization is seen as a stage, a theater in which every actor plays certain roles and attempts to communicate the right impressions to the right audiences. The main premise of this frame is that whenever reason and analysis fail to contain the dark forces of ambiguity, human beings erect symbols, myths, rituals, and ceremonies to bring order, meaning, and predictability out of chaos and confusion.

Transforming leaders are visionary leaders, and visionary leadership is invariably symbolic. Examination of symbolic leaders reveals that they follow a consistent set of practices and rules. Transforming leaders use symbols to capture attention. When a friend and colleague of mine became principal of a charter school in Philadelphia, she knew that she faced a substantial challenge. The school had all the usual problems of urban public schools: decaying physical plant, lack of student discipline, racial tension, troubles with the teaching staff, low morale, and limited resources. The only good news was that the situation was so bad that almost any change would be an improvement. In such a situation, symbolic leaders will try to do something visible, even dramatic, to let people know that changes are on the way. During the summer before she assumed her duties, my friend wrote a letter to every teacher to set up an individual meeting. She traveled to meet teachers wherever they wanted, driving two hours in one case. She asked teachers how they felt about the school and what changes they wanted.

She also felt that something needed to be done about the school building because nobody likes to work in a dumpy place. She decided that the front door and some of the worst classrooms had to be painted. She had few illusions about getting the bureaucracy of the Philadelphia public school system to provide painters, so she persuaded some of her family members to help her do the painting. When school opened, students and staff members immediately saw that things were going to be different, if only symbolically. Perhaps even more important, staff members received a subtle challenge to make a contribution themselves.

My own contribution to the situational leadership theory and the Bolman/Deal model in particular is what I call the *moral frame*. In my view, the moral frame completes situational leadership theory. Without it, leaders could just as easily use their leadership skills for promoting evil as for promoting good. Leaders operating out of the moral frame are concerned about their obligations to their followers. Moral frame leaders use some type of moral compass to direct their behavior. They practice what has been described as servant leadership and are concerned with those individuals and groups that are marginalized in their organizations and in society. In short, they are concerned about equality, fairness, and social justice. The moral frame is explored in more detail in chapter 11 (Palestini 2011).

Leadership Behaviors

Lest one be confused about what leadership behaviors fit into what frames, here are some examples:

Structural Frame Behaviors

- developing a vision
- setting goals
- developing a strategic plan

- implementing the plan
- proposing and implementing change in the form of improvements
- closely supervising followers
- developing rules and regulations
- developing job descriptions and responsibilities
- striving for the magis (continuous improvement)
- demonstrating competency (knowledgeable, organized, industrious, passionate, committed)
- hands-on managing
- attending to detail
- lifelong learning
- meticulously preparing
- behaving authoritatively
- using analytical and logical thinking
- mastering the technical aspects of one's profession

Human Resource Frame Behaviors

- developing a system of rewards to motivate employees
- giving praise for accomplishments
- empowering others
- demonstrating concern for the individual (*cura personalis*)
- engaging in participative decision making
- team building
- acknowledging special occasions (e.g., birthdays, anniversaries, get well sentiments)
- managing by walking around (being visible)

Symbolic Frame Behaviors

- displaying concern for one's personal appearance
- modeling desired behavior
- developing motivational speeches and publications
- using inspirational quotes, slogans, adages, etc. (on letterhead/posters)
- displaying symbols of achievement in the workplace
- telling stories, jokes, etc.
- being visible

Political Frame Behaviors

- negotiating a contract or covenant on compensation and working conditions
- lobbying for improvements
- fund raising and institutional development activities
- making compromises (quid pro quo)
- building political and social capital
- engaging in a force-field analysis (neutralizing opposing forces) to effect change

Moral Frame Behaviors

- developing a personal moral compass to guide one's behavior
- striving for the *magis* (the greater good)
- modeling personal integrity and moral character (being honest and forthright)
- being sensitive to the human needs of all (*cura personalis*), especially the marginalized in the workplace
- being concerned about equality, fairness, and social justice in the workplace and in society

An example of how the Bolman and Deal model plays out in practice is depicted in table 3.1.

The Hersey/Blanchard Model

In an attempt to integrate previous knowledge about leadership into a prescriptive model of leadership style, this model cites the "readiness of followers," defined as their ability and willingness to accomplish a specific task, as the major contingency that influences appropriate leadership style (Hersey and Blanchard 1988). Follower readiness incorporates the follower's level of achievement motivation, ability, and willingness to assume responsibility for his or her own behavior in accomplishing specific tasks, and education and experience relevant to the task. The model combines task and relationship behavior to yield four possible styles, as shown in figure 3.1.

Table 3.1. Bolman and Deal Leadership Model

	Structural	Human Resource	Political	Symbolic	Moral
Effective Leadership					
Leader is:	Social engineer	Catalyst, servant	Advocate	Prophet or hero	Role model
Leadership process:	Analysis, design, preparation	Support, empowerment	Advocacy, coalition building	Inspiration, framing experience	Model moral behavior
Ineffective Leadership					
Leader is:	Petty tyrant	Wimp, pushover	Con artist, hustler	Fanatic, fool	Self-righteous
Leadership process:	Management by detail and coercion	Management by abdication	Management by manipulation	Management by mirage, smoke and mirrors	Management by proselytizing

Source: Adapted from Bolman and Deal 1991.

ASSESSMENT OF THE THE LEADERSHIP BEHAVIOR

LEADER BEHAVIOR

Readiness Level III Participating Style	Readiness Level II Selling Style
Readiness Level IV Delegating Style	Readiness Level I Telling Style

FOLLOWER READINESS

R IV	R III	R II	R I
Seasoned veteran and/or very secure	much experience and/or secure	some experience and/or confident	inexperienced and/or insecure

Figure 3.1. Hersey and Blanchard Leadership Model

Leaders should use a telling style, and provide specific instructions and closely supervise performance, when followers are unable and unwilling or insecure (RI). Leaders should use a selling style, and explain decisions and provide opportunity for clarification, when followers have moderate-to-low readiness (RII). A participating style, in which the leader shares ideas and helps facilitate decision making, is useful when followers have moderate-to-high readiness (RIII). Finally, leaders should use a delegating style, and give responsibility for decisions and implementation to followers, when followers are able, willing, and confident (RIV).

Although some researchers have questioned the conceptual clarity, validity, robustness, and utility of the model, as well as the instruments used to measure leadership style, others have supported the utility of the theory. For example, the Leadership Effectiveness and Description (LEAD) Scale and related instruments, developed to measure leadership style by Hersey and Blanchard, are widely used in industrial training programs. This model can easily be adapted to educational administration and be used analytically to understand leadership deficiencies and to prescribe the appropriate style for a variety of situations.

CHAPTER 3

Transformational Leadership

Transformational leaders are situational but are also able to use their personal charisma to inspire their followers. They talk to their followers about how essential their performance is, how confident they are in the followers, how exceptional the followers are, and how he or she expects the group's performance to exceed expectations. Warren Buffett, Jack Welsh, and Bill Gates in industry, and Marie Montessori, the late Marcus Foster, and former Notre Dame president, Reverend Theodore Hesburgh in education are examples of this type of leader. Such leaders use dominance, self-confidence, a need for influence, and conviction of moral righteousness to increase their charisma and consequently their leadership effectiveness.

A transformational leader changes an organization by recognizing an opportunity and developing a vision, communicating that vision to organizational members, building trust in the vision, and achieving the vision by motivating organizational members. The leader helps subordinates recognize the need for revitalizing the organization by developing a felt need for change, overcoming resistance to change, and avoiding quick-fix solutions to problems. Encouraging subordinates to act as devil's advocates with regard to the leader, building networks outside the organization, and visiting other organizations also help them recognize a need for revitalization. The transformational leader creates a new vision and mobilizes commitment to it by planning or educating others. He or she builds trust through demonstrating personal expertise, self-confidence, and personnel integrity. Finally, the transformational leader must institutionalize the change by replacing old technical, political, cultural, and social networks with new ones.

A transformational leader motivates subordinates to achieve beyond their original expectations by increasing their awareness about the importance of designated outcomes and ways of attaining them, by getting workers to go beyond their self-interest to that of the team, the school, the school system, and the larger society, by changing or expanding the individual's needs. Subordinates report that they work harder for such leaders. In addition, such leaders are judged higher in leadership potential by their subordinates than are the more common transactional leaders.

One should be cognizant, however, of the negative side of charismatic leadership that may exist if the leader overemphasizes devotion to him- or herself, makes personal needs paramount, or uses highly effective communication skills to mislead or manipulate others. Such leaders may be so driven to achieve a vision that they ignore the costly implications of their goals. The superintendent who overexpands his or her jurisdiction in an effort to form an "empire," only to have the massive system turn into a bureaucratic nightmare, is an example of transformational leadership gone sour. Nevertheless, recent research has verified the overall effectiveness of the transformational leadership style.

An Effective Leadership Formula

For the concrete/sequential thinkers among us, it is oftentimes clearer and more understandable if a complex theory such as situational leadership theory can be placed in mathematical terms. The following is my attempt to do so:

$$\text{Effective Leadership Behavior} = (\text{is a function of}) \frac{St + Hr + Pl + Sy}{Readiness} (Moral)$$

where St stands for structural frame behavior, Hr stands for human resource behavior, Pl stands for political frame behavior, Sy stands for symbolic frame behavior, Moral stands for moral frame behavior, and Readiness stands for the maturity (the ability and willingness to perform the task) level of the follower(s).

Thus one would articulate this formula in the following manner: Effective leadership behavior is the result of or the function of the appropriate application of one or some combination of structural, human resource, political, and symbolic frame behavior, depending on the readiness level of the followers, with the moral frame being a constant.

IMPLICATIONS FOR EDUCATION

The implications of leadership theory for educational administrators are rather clear. The successful administrator needs to have a sound grasp of leadership theory and the skills to implement it. The principles of situational and transformational leadership theory are guides to effective administrative behavior. The leadership behavior applied to an inexperienced faculty member may be significantly different than that applied to a more experienced and tested one. Task behavior or structural frame behavior may be appropriate in dealing with a new teacher, while relationship behavior or human resource frame behavior may be more appropriate when dealing with a seasoned teacher.

The four frames of leadership discussed by Bolman and Deal may be particularly helpful to school administrators. Consideration of the structural, human relations, political, and symbolic implications of our leadership behavior can keep an administrator attuned to the various dimensions affecting appropriate leadership behavior. With the need to deal with collective bargaining entities, school boards, and a variety of other power issues, the political frame considerations may be particularly helpful in understanding the complexity of relationships that exist between administrators and these groups. Asking oneself the questions posed earlier under the political frame can be an effective guide to the appropriate leadership behavior in dealing with these groups. The Hersey/Blanchard model, on the other hand, may be particularly enlightening in recognizing the importance of employee readiness and the need to adapt one's leadership style to the readiness level of the follower.

Recently, a plethora of research studies have been conducted on leadership and leadership styles. The overwhelming evidence indicates that there is no one leadership style that is most appropriate in all situations. Rather, an administrator's leadership style should be adapted to the situation so that at various times task behavior or relationship behavior might be appropriate. At other times and in other situations, various degrees of both task and relationship behavior may be most effective.

The emergence of transformational leadership has seen leadership theory come full circle. Transformational leadership theory combines aspects of the early trait theory perspective with the more current situational or contingency models. The personal charisma of the leader, along with his or her ability to formulate an educational vision and to communicate it to others, determines the transformational leader's effectiveness.

Since the effective leader is expected to adapt his or her leadership style to an ever-changing environment, administration becomes an even more complex and challenging task. However, a thorough knowledge of leadership theory can make some sense of the apparent chaos that the administrator faces on an almost daily basis.

DIAGNOSTIC CHECKLIST

Here are some questions that may be helpful in assessing the effectiveness of the leadership in your institution:

- Do the administrators display the necessary behaviors required for effective leadership?
- Do the leaders encourage the appropriate amount of participation in decision making?
- Does the leadership adapt their leadership behavior to the readiness levels of the followers?
- Are the leaders transformational, seeking continuous improvement?
- Do leaders operate in all five frames of organizational leadership?

4

ONE-MINUTE ASSESSMENT OF THE MOTIVATION PROCESS

Neither regulations nor resources, neither technical innovations nor program reorganizations, can significantly alter school performance if the teacher motivation system fails to energize and shape teacher behavior in ways that link educational program requirements to student learning needs.

—Douglas E. Mitchell, Flora Ida Ortiz, and Tedi K. Mitchell

Blanchard and Johnson suggest that managers utilize praising and reprimanding as motivational devices in an organization. This flows from their first "secret" of effective management, goal setting. Goal-setting theory suggests that setting difficult but attainable goals that are mutually agreed upon can be a powerful motivator (Blanchard and Johnson 1982). Setting goals like higher reading scores on standardized tests or lower teacher absenteeism or a higher graduation rate help focus behavior and motivate individuals to achieve the desired end. However, in order for goal setting to be an effective motivator, the individual involved needs feedback on whether movement toward attaining the goal is adequately progressing.

This is where one-minute praisings and reprimands come in. It is important that the administrator keep his or her staff abreast of the adequacy of their performance. When they are very specific and clear, both praise and reprimands can be effective sources of motivation. As Blanchard and Johnson point out, however, one should "never attack a person's worth or value as a person" (1982, 17).

Reprimand the behavior only, not the person. Thus, the feedback and the individual's reaction to it are about the specific behavior and not their feelings about themselves as human beings. It is always a good idea to follow or precede a reprimand with praise. Make certain that the staff member knows that his or her behavior is not okay, but that he or she is okay. In religious terms, we are advised to "hate the sin and love the sinner." According to Blanchard and Johnson, the one-minute manager should not be Nice 'n' Tough, but rather, Tough 'n' Nice (1982, 32).

Reinforcement theory applies behaviorist learning theories to motivation and has implications for the effectiveness of praise and reprimands (Thorndike 1924). This theory emphasizes the importance of feedback and rewards in motivating desired behavior through diverse reinforcement techniques, including positive reinforcement, like praise, and negative reinforcement, like reprimands.

Positive reinforcement involves actively encouraging a desired behavior by repeatedly praising desired behaviors or outcomes with rewards or feedback. This feedback "shapes" behavior by encouraging the reinforced or rewarded behavior to recur. If the behavior is not precisely what is desired by the administrator, repeated reinforcements resulting in successive approximations of the desired behavior can move the actual behavior closer to the desired behavior. For example, if a principal desires more interactive classroom instruction of a teacher, the principal might compliment the teacher when a cooperative learning activity is part of the lesson plan, and when other interactive techniques are used, additional praise may be given. Praise and other incentives are used until the best performance occurs.

Punishment, on the other hand, actively reduces undesirable behaviors by applying an undesirable reinforcer (reprimand) to an undesirable behavior. Although it can be effective in eliminating undesirable behavior, punishment can produce anger and bitterness and be counterproductive in the long run. This is why the administrator must be careful to reprimand infrequently, and when doing so, to reprimand the undesirable behavior and not the individual. It is also the reason why, when possible, a reprimand of the behavior should be followed or preceded by praising the individual. "Your lesson plan for today was somewhat poorly conceived, but I know that you have the ability to do better" is an example of reprimanding the behavior and praising the individual. Goal-setting theory and praising and reprimanding are just two of the ways to motivate faculty and staff. There are a number of other ways of doing so.

NEEDS THEORIES

Suppose the president of a college makes $200,000 a year and a typical faculty member earns $100,000. And suppose this college decided to base part of its annual salary increases on whether the college met its recruitment quota. Why would such a college think this policy might motivate its employees? Early motivation theorists would explain such a situation by saying that the college expects the new policy to meet the employees' *needs*—their basic requirements for living and working productively.

How do we identify employees' needs? To do a good job of identifying them, we probably would need to spend a great deal of time talking with the employees and observing their behavior both in and out of the work environment. Many times, determining employees' needs outside of the work environment is conjecture. In the example given earlier, we might conjecture that such a policy might meet the employees' achievement motive.

In this section, we present, in brief, two of the most popular needs theories: Maslow's hierarchy-of-needs theory and William Glasser's control theory. Each of these theories describes a specific set of needs the researchers believe individuals have, and each differs somewhat in the number and kinds of needs identified.

Maslow's Hierarchy of Needs

In 1935, Abraham Maslow developed the first needs theory, and it is still one of the most popular and well-known motivation theories. Maslow stated that individuals have five needs, arranged in a hierarchy from the most basic to the highest level, as shown in figure 4.1: physiological, safety and security, belongingness and love, esteem, and self-actualization (Maslow 1987).

CHAPTER 4

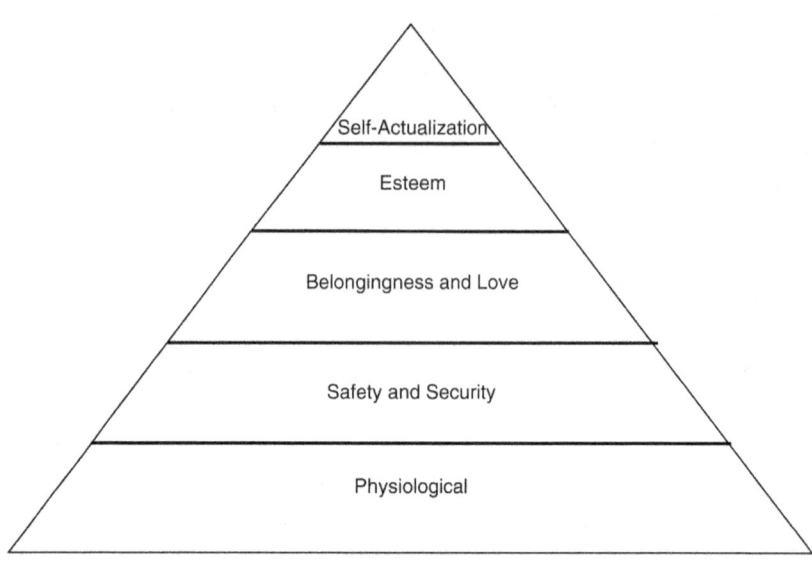

Lowest unsatisfied need becomes the most powerful and significant need.

Figure 4.1. Maslow's Pyramid

Physiological needs are the most basic needs an individual has. These include, at a minimum, a person's requirement for food, water, shelter, and the ability to care for his or her family. Providing employees with a living wage and medical and dental coverage would help satisfy this need. Safety needs include a person's desire for security or protection. This translates most directly into concerns for short-term and long-term job security, as well as physical safety at work. Belongingness and love needs focus on the social aspects of work and nonworking situations.

Virtually all individuals desire affectionate relationships or regular interaction with others, which can become a key facet of job design. Esteem needs relate to a person's desire to master his or her work, demonstrate competence, build a reputation as an outstanding performer, hold a position of prestige, receive public recognition, and feel self-confident. Self-actualization needs reflect an individual's desire to grow and develop to his or her fullest potential. An individual often wants the opportunity to be creative on the job or desires autonomy, responsibility, and challenge.

According to needs theory, organizations must meet unsatisfied needs in order to motivate their employees. In Maslow's scheme, the lowest unsatisfied need, starting with the basic physiological needs and continuing through safety, belonging and love, esteem, and self-actualization needs, becomes the prepotent or most powerful and significant need. Although the order may vary in certain special circumstances, generally the prepotent need motivates an individual to act to fulfill it; satisfied needs do not motivate. If, for example, a person lacks sufficient food and clothing, he or she will act to satisfy those basic physiological needs; hence, this person would most likely work to receive pay or other benefits to satisfy those needs. On the other hand, a person whose physiological, safety, and belongingness needs are satisfied will be motivated to satisfy needs at the next level, the esteem needs. For this person, performance is motivated not by pay, but by increased esteem, by a promotion or other changes in a job's title or status.

Consider again the example of the college that attached some of the salary increases to whether the college reached its recruitment goals. Using Maslow's theory to diagnose the likely effectiveness of the new policy, we can ask three questions: (1) Which needs have already been satisfied? (2) Which unsatisfied need is lowest in the hierarchy? (3) Can those needs be satisfied with the new policy? If, for example, the physiological and safety needs have been satisfied, then the social needs become prepotent; if the new policy can satisfy those needs, which is unlikely, then, according to Maslow's theory, it would be motivating. In our example, then, it is likely that the new policy would satisfy the teachers' and administrators' achievement or self-esteem needs.

Control Theory

William Glasser suggests that individuals strive to gain control over their emotions and behavior so that they will have healthier and more productive lives. His control theory posits that individuals are born with five basic human needs: survival, love, power, fun, and freedom. These needs must be satisfied in order for individuals to be productive in their work and private lives. According to Glasser, people need to control their own behavior so as to make the most need-satisfying choices possible.

The survival need is the innate desire of individuals to be safe and secure. Love and belonging refer to the need for affiliation and affirmation. Power is the need to obtain knowledge and expertise. To Glasser, knowledge is power. Our inalienable right to the pursuit of happiness is our effort to fulfill the need for fun. And the opportunity to make free choices is what Glasser believes satisfies our need for freedom (Glasser 1984).

According to Glasser, effective managers will see that these five needs are satisfied if his or her employees are expected to be productive. Coercion and competition are counterproductive. Quality performance, therefore, cannot be achieved in an adversarial setting. Workers will perform if coerced, but they will not perform in a quality manner. Competition enables one person to succeed while others fail. Cooperation, on the other hand, allows many winners.

Although Glasser's control theory has not been verified by empirical research, it has been demonstrated to be successful in a number of school system settings including the Johnson City, New York, school district, where standardized achievement test scores increased dramatically while Glasser's techniques were being used. The faculty was also judged to be more productive when programs were implemented that satisfied the five basic needs.

UTILIZATION OF NEEDS THEORIES

Despite some caveats, needs theory can be utilized effectively in educational settings. When an administrator is developing or refining the overall school program and organizational goals, he or she should analyze each component with the various needs in mind to be certain that some aspect of the activity or policy addresses one or more of our common needs. For example, if a teacher is preparing a lesson, he or she should go through Glasser's or another theorist's needs, to see if the lesson addresses the learner's needs for survival, love, power, fun, and freedom. In the same way, if an administrator is implementing a Total Quality Management initiative or some other organizational development program at his or her institution, the administrator should incorporate facets that would satisfy each of the faculty and staff's needs in some significant way.

Goal-Setting Theory

Although extensive research has been conducted on the goal-setting process and its relationship to performance, in this section we highlight only a sample of the findings. Goals, which any member of an organization can set, describe a desired future state, such as lower absenteeism, higher standardized test scores, higher teacher and staff satisfaction, or specified performance levels. Once established, they can focus behavior and motivate individuals to achieve the desired end state (Vance and Colella 1990).

Goals can vary in at least three ways: specificity, difficulty, and acceptance. The specificity or clarity of goals refers to the extent to which their accomplishment is observable and measurable. "Reducing absenteeism by 20 percent" is a highly specific goal for a school; "all children achieving" is a much less specific goal. Goal difficulty, or the level of performance desired, can also vary significantly. A superintendent of schools might set a goal to recruit 10 percent more of the school-aged children in his or her school district or to increase standardized test scores by 10 percent; the first goal might be relatively easy, the second extremely difficult.

Although goal-setting research originally called for setting moderately difficult goals, now empirical studies indicate that a linear relationship exists between goal difficulty and performance. Empirical studies that combined the two characteristics of goal specificity and difficulty showed that performances accompanying specific difficult goals were better than those accompanying vague, non-quantitative ones. Individuals' acceptance of stated goals, or their commitment to accomplishing the goals, may vary. In general, a subordinate is less likely to accept a goal as his or her own and try to accomplish it if a manager assigns the goal rather than jointly sets it with the subordinate (Latham and Yukl 1975).

Redesign of Work

Work redesign modifies specific jobs to increase both the quality of the employees' work experience and the performance. Jobs, as a central concern in work design, are defined simply as a set of tasks grouped together under one job title; for example, teacher, principal, dean, and custodian are designed to be performed by a single individual. Moreover, jobs are bureaucratic, they are part of the organization, they exist independently of job incumbents, and they are relatively static. Jobs do change, but not on a day-to-day basis. As a strategy for motivation and change, then, work-redesign programs alter the content and process of jobs to match the work motivation of individuals. That is, work-redesign efforts modify the school organization to enhance educator and student motivation. The approach to work redesign that will be considered here is career ladders.

Career Ladders

As a redesign of educational work, career-ladder programs are seen by many policy makers as moving teaching careers closer to the professional end of the occupational continuum. Career ladders became one of the most touted and widely mandated reforms of teaching and schools during the 1980s and remnants of it continue to exist today.

Three reasons are generally offered as rationale for creating career-ladder programs. The first is based on the research finding that many of the best teachers leave their instructional careers after a brief foray in the classroom. Historically, about 50 percent of a teacher cohort will leave teaching during the first six years. Moreover, a disproportionate percentage of those leaving teaching are the most talented. The second reason given for redesign is based on the observation that teaching in the elementary and secondary schools has a flat career path. Teachers have limited opportunities for advancement in their instructional work. New and experienced teachers have the same role expectations. Teachers with motivations to advance or gain new responsibilities generally have two choices; they can remain frustrated in their self-contained classrooms or they can leave. A third reason supporting the need for career ladders is that, although teaching is demanding work requiring creativity and versatility, it is repetitive. Despite the variety of classroom challenges and achievements, one year can look very much like the next and there is little prospect to change the year-to-year pattern. Hence, career-ladder programs were seen as ways to attract and retain highly talented individuals to education (Hart 1987).

A career-ladder program redesigns jobs to provide individuals with prospects for promotion, formalizes status ranks for teachers, matches teacher abilities with job tasks, and shares the responsibilities for school and faculty improvements with the professional staff. In essence, the goal of career-ladder programs is to enrich work and enlarge teacher responsibilities. Career ladders, as job-enrichment models, generally include promotions to higher ranks with the assumption of additional duties at each higher step. For example, mentoring and supervising new teachers, developing curriculum materials, and evaluating programs are typical. A more creative and attractive version of a career ladder is to provide teachers with an avenue to obtaining their doctorates so they can move to higher education later in their careers.

DIAGNOSTIC CHECKLIST

Here are some questions that might be addressed in assessing your institution's motivational processes:

- Do the rewards provided satisfy the variety of individual needs?
- Is a full range of motivational tools being used?
- Are rewards both internal and external?
- Are they applied equitably and consistently?
- Is reinforcement theory (praising and reprimanding) being employed effectively?
- Do individuals set goals as a source of motivation (goal-setting theory)?
- Are the rewards and incentives effective in motivating desired behaviors?

5

ONE-MINUTE ASSESSMENT OF THE COMMUNICATION PROCESS

It appears then that genuine friendship cannot exist where one of the parties is unwilling to hear the truth and the other is equally indisposed to speak it.

—*Cicero*

One of the perennial complaints of school personnel is a lack of communication between themselves and another segment of the school community. Oftentimes, the greatest perceived "communications gap" is between the faculty and the administration. If an administrator is to be effective, then, he or she must master the skill of effective communication.

THE VALUE OF FEEDBACK

Feedback is perhaps the most important aspect of an effective communications process. Feedback refers to an acknowledgment by the receiver that the message has been received; it provides the sender with information about the receiver's understanding of the message being sent.

Often one-way communication occurs between administrators and their colleagues. Because of inherent power differences in their positions, administrators may give large quantities of information and directions to their faculty and staff without providing the opportunity for them to show their understanding or receipt of the information. These managers often experience conflict between their role as authorities and a desire to be liked and trusted by their colleagues. Other administrators have relied almost exclusively on written memoranda posted on the faculty/staff bulletin board as a way of communicating. In addition to the inherent lack of feedback involved in this format, the use of a single channel of communication also limits the effectiveness of communication. The proliferation of the use of email has alleviated this problem somewhat by providing a relatively facile feedback mechanism. Encouraging feedback from others, however, helps show them that you are concerned about them as individuals, in ways that go beyond merely ensuring that they produce.

COMMUNICATIONS DEVICES

What can individuals do to improve their communication in both formal and informal settings? In this section we examine three ways of increasing communication effectiveness: creating a supportive communication climate; using an assertive communication style; and using active listening techniques.

In communicating with their faculties and staffs, administrators know they must create a trusting and supportive environment. Creating such a climate has the objective of shifting from attribution or blaming to problem solving and staff development. Administrators must thus avoid making employees feel defensive, that is, threatened by the communication. They can create such an atmosphere in at least six tried and true ways (Zuker 1983, 79):

1. They use descriptive rather than evaluative speech and do not imply that the receiver needs to change. An administrator may describe teacher traits in terms of strengths and areas in need of further development, rather than describing them as weaknesses.
2. They take a clinical approach, which implies a desire to collaborate in exploring a mutual problem, rather than trying to control or change

ASSESSMENT OF THE COMMUNICATION PROCESS

the listener. An administrator can ask the teacher what he or she hopes to achieve in the lesson, or for the academic year, rather than setting out a list of preordained goals for the teacher.

3. They are spontaneous and honest, and reveal their goals, rather than appearing to use "strategy" that involves ambiguous and multiple motivations. A superintendent might share with the school community the need for restructuring and possible areas of downsizing rather than doing so surreptitiously, for example.
4. They convey empathy for the feelings of their listener, rather than appearing unconcerned or neutral about the listener's welfare. They give reassurance that they are identifying with the listener's problems, rather than denying the legitimacy of the problems. For example, when reviewing a union grievance with a teacher, the principal may indicate sensitivity to the teacher's position even though the decision may ultimately go against the teacher.
5. They indicate that they feel equal rather than superior to the listener. Thus they suggest that they will enter a shared relationship, not simply dominate the interaction. A college dean may come out from behind his or her desk and sit next to a colleague to indicate a relationship of equality.
6. Finally, they communicate that they will be flexible regarding their own behavior and ideas, rather than be dogmatic about them. They do not give the impression that they know all the answers and do not need help from anyone. An administrator can concede that he or she does not know if his or her suggestion will work, but ask that the employee in question "try it."

Another tested way of improving interpersonal communication is by encouraging individuals to communicate using as complete knowledge of themselves and others as possible. The Johari window provides an analytical tool that individuals can use to identify information that is available for use in communication. Figure 5.1 illustrates this model of interpersonal knowledge (Gordon 1993). Note that information about an individual is represented along two dimensions: (1) information known and unknown by the self and (2) information known and unknown by others.

	Known by Self	Unknown by Self
Known by Others	Open self	Blind self
Unknown by Others	Concealed self	Unknown self

Figure 5.1. Johari Window

Together these dimensions form a four-category representation of the individual. The open self is information known by the self and known by others. The blind self is information unknown by the self and known by others, such as others' perceptions of your behavior or attitudes. The concealed self is information known by you and unknown by others; secrets we keep from others about ourselves fall into this category. Finally, the unconscious self is information that is unknown to the self and unknown to others. To ensure quality communication, in most cases an individual should communicate from his or her "open self" to another's open self and limit the amount of information concealed or in the blind spot. Guarded communication may be appropriate, however, if one party has violated trust in the past, if the parties have an adversarial relationship, or if the relationship is transitory.

The Assertive Communication Style

An assertive style, which is honest, direct, and firm, also improves communication. With this style a person expresses personal needs, opinions, and feelings in honest and direct ways and stands up for his or her rights without violating the other person's rights. Assertive behavior is reflected in the content and the nonverbal style of the message. The assertive leader, for example, is clear and direct when explaining work to subordinates, doesn't hover, and criticizes fairly, objectively, and constructively.

Consider the situation of a superintendent whose assistant has missed two important deadlines in the past month. How would she respond assertively? She might say to her assistant: "I know you missed the last two deadlines. Is there an explanation I should know? It is important that you meet the next deadlines." An assertive response can include the expression of anger, frustration, or disappointment, but is couched in terms that would allow for feedback to obtain the employee's explanation for the behavior.

We can further contrast the assertive approach to nonassertive and aggressive styles. Nonassertive communication describes behavior where the sender does not stand up for his or her leadership responsibilities and indicates that his or her feelings are unimportant; the person may be hesitant, apologetic, or fearful. In the situation of a missed deadline, nonassertive behavior might involve saying nothing to your assistant, hoping the situation would not recur. Individuals act nonassertively because they may mistake assertion for aggression, mistake nonassertion for politeness or being helpful, refuse to accept their leadership responsibilities, experience anxiety about negative consequences of assertiveness, or lack assertiveness skills (Palestini 2012).

In aggressive communication one expresses one's view and rights without respecting the rights of the other person. Aggressive behavior attempts to dominate and control others by sounding accusing or superior. In the situation of the missed deadlines, an aggressive response might be "You always miss deadlines. You're taking advantage of me and the situation. If you miss another deadline, disciplinary action will be taken." While such a response may result in the desired behavior in the short run, its long-term consequences likely will be dysfunctional, resulting in distrust between the individuals involved. Ultimately, such behavior will negatively affect productivity and will especially affect the submission of creative and innovative solutions offered to management by the employee.

Using Active Listening Techniques

Active listening, which requires understanding both the content and the intent of a message, can be facilitated by paraphrasing, perception checking, and behavior description. The receiver can paraphrase the message conveyed by the sender by stating in his or her own way what the other person's remarks convey. For example, if the sender states, "I don't like the work I am doing," the receiver might paraphrase it as "Are you saying that you are dissatisfied with the profession of education?" or "Are you dissatisfied with the grade that you teach?" or "Do you wish to be reassigned to another school?" Note that these ways of paraphrasing the original message suggest very different understandings of the original statement. The sender, upon receiving this feedback from the receiver, can then clarify his or her meaning.

Alternatively, the receiver may perception check; that is, describe what he or she perceives as the sender's inner state at the time of communication to check his or her understanding of the message. For example, if the sender states, "I don't like the work I am doing," the receiver might check his or her perception of the statement by asking, "Are you dissatisfied with the tasks you have been given?" "Are you dissatisfied by the way you are being treated?" or, "Are you dissatisfied with me as a supervisor?" Note that answers to these questions will identify different feelings.

A third way of checking communication is through behavior description. Here the individual reports specific, observable actions of others without making accusations or generalizations about their motives, personality, or characteristics. Similarly, description of feelings, where the individual specifies or identifies feelings by name, analogy, or some other verbal representation, can increase active listening. For example, in the instance cited above, you might observe of the speaker, "You look angry," "You look resentful," or "You seem bitter."

EXTERNAL COMMUNICATION

As we have seen in chapter 1, the open system model of organizational structure highlights the vulnerability and interdependence of organizations and their environments. External environments are important because they affect the internal structures and processes of organizations; hence, one is forced to look both inside and outside the organization to explain behavior within school organizations. However, the growing necessity to interact with the outside environment places added responsibilities and demands on the school district's communications processes. The need to communicate with parents, government officials, advocacy groups, and the mass media cannot be denied. This necessity, however, is a relatively recent phenomenon and presents difficulties to administrators whose training does not normally include communicating with the public through the mass media.

Although the principles of effective communication still prevail when dealing with the outside community, some nuances need to be stressed. Perhaps the most important aspect of communication that needs to be considered when dealing with the public is the uniformity of the message.

The message must be clear and consistent and be emanating from a singular source. In these cases, the "chain of command" and "channels of communication" need to be well-defined and structured along the lines of the classical model. It is imperative that the school "speak with one voice." Someone in the school district should be designated as the clearing house for all external communication. This individual, or office, should review all external communication for clarity and accuracy and school personnel should be keenly aware of the school's policy with regard to external communication. Thus, although a more loosely structured communication system is very appropriate for internal communications, a more tightly structured one is necessary for effective external communications.

MATRIX DESIGN

To overcome some of the problems of the classical chain of command structure of most organizations, including schools, matrix or mixed designs have evolved to improve mechanisms of lateral communication and information flow across the organization (Lewis 1987).

The matrix organization, originally developed in the aerospace industry, is characterized by a dual authority system. There are usually functional and program or product line managers, both reporting to a common superior and both exercising authority over workers within the matrix. Typically, a matrix organization is particularly useful in highly specialized technological areas that focus on innovation. Thus, schools, school systems, and institutions of higher education make ideal settings for matrix designs. Especially in interdisciplinary academic programs, the matrix structure facilitates the coordination of the team and allows team members to contribute their special expertise.

The matrix design has some disadvantages that stem from the dual authority lines. Individual workers may find having two supervisors to be untenable since it can create conflicting expectations and ambiguity. The matrix design may also be expensive in that both functional and program managers may spend a considerable amount of time at meetings attempting to keep everyone informed of program activities. A matrix design in a college setting is depicted in figure 5.2.

CHAPTER 5

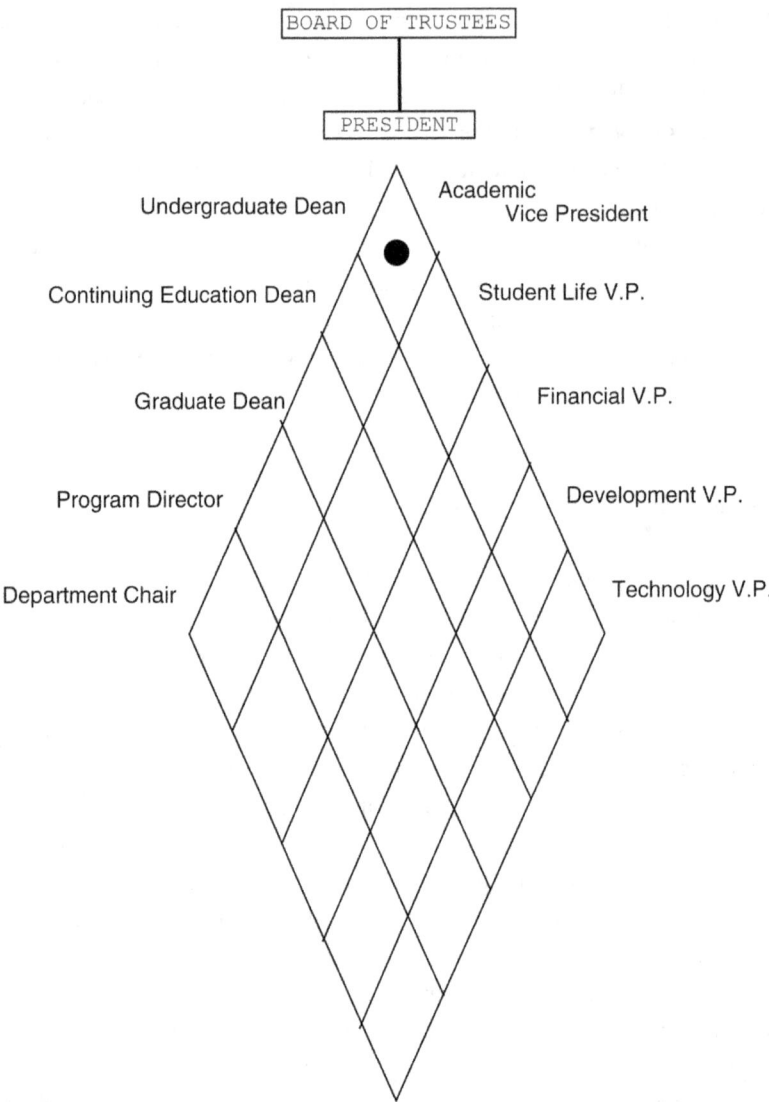

Figure 5.2. Matrix Design

The use of matrix design in education is not very common, but it is a viable way of organizing when communication needs to occur outside the "proper channels." The popularity of interdisciplinary and multicultural courses and programs in education has caused an increased interest in matrix design. Many high schools and colleges are informally organized in a matrix design. It would most likely serve these institutions well to consider it as a formal organizational structure, especially in cases when communication problems are evident.

CONCLUSION

A foreign-born plumber in New York once wrote to the Bureau of Standards that he found hydrochloric acid fine for cleaning drains, and he asked if they agreed. Washington replied: "The efficacy of hydrochloric acid is indisputable, but the chlorine residue is incompatible with metallic permanence." The plumber wrote back that he was mighty glad the Bureau agreed with him. Considerably alarmed, the Bureau replied a second time: "We cannot assume responsibility for the production of toxic and noxious residues with hydrochloric acid, and suggest that you use an alternative procedure." The plumber was happy to learn that the Bureau still agreed with him. Whereupon Washington wrote: "Don't use hydrochloric acid; it eats the hell out of pipes."

Communication with ease and clarity is no simple task. There are, however, various orientations toward how it can be most effectively carried out. Classical theory, social system theory, and open system theory (chapter 1) all incorporate a perspective toward the communication process; or, who should say what through which channel to whom and to what effect. Classical theory stresses that the communication process exists to facilitate the manager's command and control over the employees in a formal, hierarchical, and downwardly directed manner. The purpose is to increase efficiency and productivity.

The social system orientation suggests that to be effective, communication has to be two-way and that the meaning of the message is as much to be found in the psychological makeup of the receiver as it is in the sender. The open system orientation emphasizes the communication process working toward drawing the various subsystems of an organization into a collaborating whole. Also, drawing the organization's actions into a close fit with the needs of its environment is an essential outcome of the process. This orientation emphasizes that between senders and receivers, the communication process must penetrate social class differences, cultural values, time orientations, and ethnocentrism of all types.

None of the conceptual frameworks, by itself, escapes the barriers to communication. The story of the plumber illustrates the problems of message coding, decoding, and transmission. We have suggested that in order for communication to be effective, we should adapt the process to the situation. We have suggested that when communicating with the outside community, a more structured process may be appropriate, while when communicating with the inside community a less structured process might be more appropriate. This approach is in concert with one of the underlying themes of this book, that, whether we are speaking about organizational structure, leadership, motivation, or communication, we need to adapt the approach or model to the situation in which we find ourselves. Taking a minute each day to obtain feedback regarding the effectiveness of the communication process at an institution is time well spent and will go a long way to ensuring a healthy organizational environment.

DIAGNOSTIC CHECKLIST

Here are some questions that may help in assessing an institution's communication process:

- How effective is the communication process?
- What barriers to communication exist?
- Is the correct communication style utilized under the proper conditions?
- Does communication include feedback, where appropriate?
- Is there a climate of mutual trust and respect?
- Are active listening and other techniques that improve the communication process used?
- Do individuals use assertive, nonassertive, or aggressive communication?

ONE-MINUTE ASSESSMENT OF THE DECISION-MAKING PROCESS

The fine art of executive decision making consists in not deciding questions that are not now pertinent, in not deciding prematurely, in not making decisions that cannot be made effective, and in not making decisions that others should make.

—*Chester I. Barnard*

Suppose Will Smith was appointed to the position of superintendent of schools for the Rose Tree School District with the expressed purpose of right-sizing the school district in light of its declining student population. Having been successful in a similar situation in another school district, how should Will Smith proceed?

There are two aspects that Will must immediately bring to the fore in the decision-making process, namely the decision's *quality* and its *acceptance*. A high-quality decision brings about the desired result while meeting relevant criteria and constraints. What would constitute a high-quality decision in the situation in Rose Tree School District? Certainly a decision that reduces costs while maintaining educational quality would be considered a high-quality one. Also, a decision that met the needs of those affected by the decision, including students, faculty, staff, administrators, and the taxpayers would qualify; so too would a decision that meets the financial, human, time, and other constraints existing in the situation.

The quality of the decision depends in part on the level of the decision maker's technical or task skills, interpersonal or leadership skills, and decision-making skills. Technical or task skills refer to the individual's knowledge of the particular area in which the decision is being made. In the decision that Will Smith must make about right-sizing, task skills refer to a knowledge of labor costs, projected revenues, educational product information, school system overhead costs, and past experience. Interpersonal or leadership skills relate to the way individuals lead, communicate with, motivate, and influence others. Will Smith, for example, must be able to convince the other stakeholders in the school system to accept the decision for which he is responsible.

Will Smith and any advisors he involves in the decision-making process must produce a decision that they and the rest of the school system community can accept, one that they are willing to "live with." For example, closing two of the schools may be a high-quality decision, but the teachers' union may oppose it so vehemently that the decision may be inoperable. Alternatively, reducing the teaching staff and increasing class size may be a high-quality decision, but parents might resist the change because they feel that their children are not receiving a quality education. Thus, "acceptance" of the decision by the stakeholders is a characteristic that needs to be considered along with the "quality" of the decision.

VROOM/YETTON DECISION-MAKING MODEL

The administrative and organizational theory literature is in agreement about the two most important factors to be considered in determining the decision style that will produce the most effective decisions. While Vroom and Yetton's model includes the additional dimensions of shared goals and conflict possibility, the two key elements are the "quality" and the "acceptance" of the decision, as described above. Figure 6.1 summarizes the identification of the decision style that is most appropriate for particular problem types (Vroom and Yetton 1973).

ASSESSMENT OF THE DECISION-MAKING PROCESS

(1) Quality (Q) - The extent to which one solution is likely to be better than another

(2) Acceptance (A) - The extent to which acceptance or commitment on the part of subordinates is crucial to the effective implementation of the decision

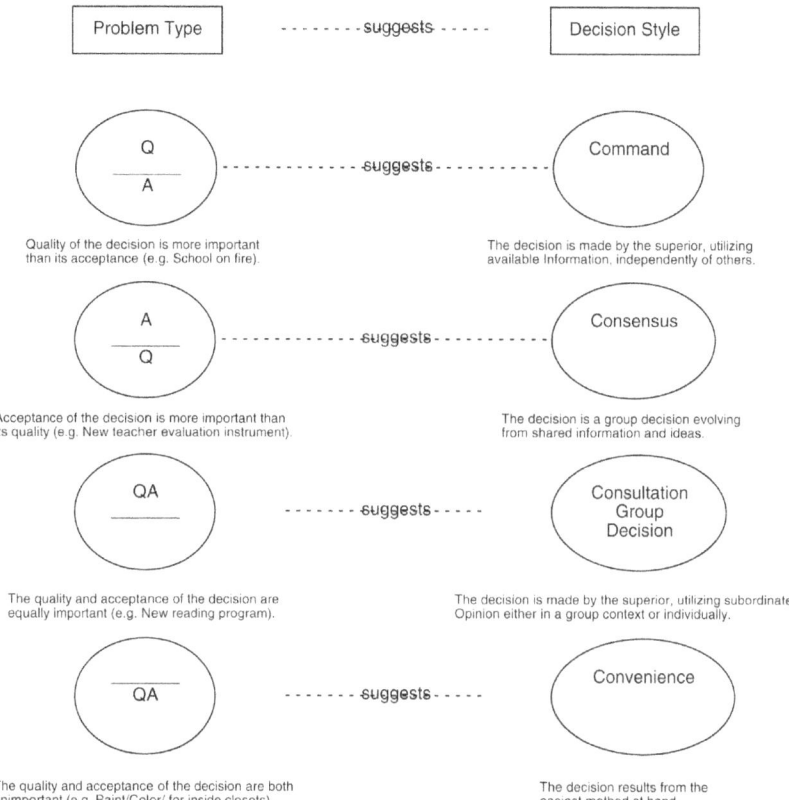

Figure 6.1. Vroom/Yetton Decision-making Model

The two key elements are "quality," or the likelihood of one decision to be more rational and right than another, and "acceptance," or the extent to which acceptance or commitment on the part of stakeholders is crucial to the effective implementation of the decision.

For example, if a new law is passed regarding the education of students with disabilities and the administrator has to decide how to communicate this to the school community, the quality of the decision would be more important than its acceptance. Therefore, the appropriate decision style is "command." On the other hand, if acceptance is more important than quality, as in the development of a new teacher evaluation instrument, the proper decision style would be "consensus."

If the quality and acceptance are of equal importance, like whether to adopt a whole language approach to reading instruction, consultation or group decision making would be the appropriate style. Finally, if neither the quality nor the acceptance is important, like deciding what color to paint the inside of the school closets, convenience would be the applicable style.

ETHICAL DECISION MAKING

In addition to evaluating a decision in terms of its quality and acceptance, we can also assess how well it meets the criterion of ethical fairness and justice. Consider, for example, a disastrous decrease in standardized test scores in a certain high school. Top administrators are faced with the decision of whether to risk public outrage and the possible transfer of significant numbers of students or to ignore the situation.

Administrators and staff can assess whether the decisions they make are ethical by applying personal moral codes or society's codes of values; they can apply philosophical views of ethical behavior; or they can assess the potential harmful consequences of behaviors to certain constituencies. A valuable tool in the ethical decision-making process could be the application of the Ignation Vision alluded to in chapter 11, especially the discernment, *cura personalis*, and social justice aspects of the vision (Rest 1986).

GROUP DECISION MAKING

The decision-making processes described thus far can apply to decisions made by individuals or groups. Yet, group decision making brings different resources to the task situation than does individual decision making. When a group makes a decision, a synergy occurs that oftentimes causes the group decision to be better than the sum of the individual decisions. The involvement of more than one individual brings additional knowledge and skills to the decision, and it tends to result in higher-quality decisions. However, the same caveat holds for decision making as we have reiterated throughout this book. That is, decision making is situational, and the idiosyncrasies of the moment dictate the decision-making approach to be taken. For example, if your school building is on fire, participative decision making is obviously not appropriate.

GROUP DIVERSITY

As the group becomes more diverse—attitudinally, behaviorally, and culturally—the advantages of diversity increase. Diversity provides the greatest asset for teams with difficult, discretionary tasks requiring innovation. Diversity becomes least helpful when working on simple tasks involving repetitive and routine procedures. Thus, when establishing a committee or task force to address a complex problem, be certain that its membership reflects the various components of the school community.

TIME REQUIRED

Group decision making generally takes more time than individual decision making. The exchange of information among many individuals, as well as effort spent on obtaining consensus, is time consuming. Sometimes, to reach a decision more quickly or to reach a decision all group members will accept, groups "satisfice" rather than optimize. That is, they tend to make decisions that are expedient (Simon 1960).

RISKINESS OF DECISIONS

There is much research to suggest that groups tend to make riskier decisions. Because no single person shoulders the consequences of the decision made by a group, individuals may feel less accountable and will accept more risky or extreme solutions. When a problem occurs in a school, the parents do not complain to the committee, they complain to the principal. Thus, a committee feels free to make a decision that is more risky.

GROUPTHINK

Irving Janis first identified groupthink as a factor that influenced the misguided 1961 Bay of Pigs invasion. The symptoms of groupthink arise when members of decision-making groups try to avoid being too critical in their judgment of other group members' ideas and focus too heavily on developing concurrence. It occurs most frequently in highly cohesive groups, particularly in stressful situations. For example, group members experiencing groupthink may feel invulnerable to criticism and hence believe that any action they take or decision they make will be positively received. They may also ignore external criticism, choosing instead to rationalize their actions or decisions as optimum. Some group members may also pressure other group members to agree with the group's decision; deviant opinions are either ignored or not tolerated; members can neither question views offered nor offer disconfirming information. All of these aspects were present in the Bay of Pigs decision (Gordon 1993).

The Bay of Pigs decision can be contrasted with John F. Kennedy's Cuban Missile Crisis decision that was made a few years later. In this case, Kennedy learned from the Bay of Pigs mistake and did not allow groupthink to influence the decision-making process, thus yielding dramatically different results.

CHOOSING GROUP DECISION MAKING

The rule of thumb regarding the use of group decision making is that unless the "acceptance" of the decision is irrelevant, some type of group decision-making process should be used. Group decision making is superior when a task or problem requires a variety of expertise, when problems have multiple parts that can be addressed by a division of labor, and when problems require estimates. Individual decision making results in more efficiency if policy dictates the correct solution. Individual decision making also tends to lead to more effective decisions for problems that require completion of a series of complex stages, so long as the individual receives input from many sources, because it allows better coordination of the phases in solving the problem. In Rose Tree School District, for example, the main decision that Will Smith and his colleagues must make is how to reduce costs without reducing quality. This type of problem requires diverse knowledge and skills, creativity, and completion of a series of complex stages, calling most likely for a combination of individual and group decision making.

Group decision making more often leads to acceptance than does decision making by individuals. In addition, since individuals involved in making a decision generally become committed to the decision, use of group consensus expedites acceptance of the decision by the group, thereby increasing individual and group commitment to the decision. Acceptance of the decision about right-sizing at Rose Tree may affect its implementation in the short run, and since school employees cannot easily be replaced, may also affect it in the long run. Therefore, the acceptance is as important as the quality of the decision.

Group decision making generally leads to higher-quality solutions unless an individual's expertise in the decision areas is identified in the beginning. At Rose Tree, Will Smith has had successful experience in right-sizing; therefore, he has less need for group input to make a high-quality decision. However, he needs the input because the acceptance of the decision is so important.

The amount of time available will determine whether group problem solving is feasible because group decision making takes much more time than individual decision making. Rose Tree School District must resolve its problem in a timely manner or risk a taxpayer revolt; therefore, the amount of group participation may be somewhat limited.

WAYS TO IMPROVE DECISION MAKING

How can decision makers overcome barriers, reduce biases, and make more effective decisions? There are at least three techniques that can improve decision making: brainstorming, the nominal group technique, the Delphi technique.

CHAPTER 6

Brainstorming

Groups or individuals use brainstorming when creativity is needed to generate many alternatives for consideration in decision making. In brainstorming, they list as many alternatives as possible without simultaneously evaluating the feasibility of any alternative. For example, Will Smith might charge a task force with listing all the ways of reducing costs in the Rose Tree School District. The absence of evaluation encourages group members to generate rather than defend ideas. Then, after ideas have been generated, they are evaluated, and decisions are made. Although brainstorming can result in many shallow and useless ideas, it can also motivate members to offer new ideas. It works best when individuals have a common view of what constitutes a good idea, but it is harder to use when specialized knowledge or complex implementation is required (Adams 1986).

Nominal Group Technique

The nominal group technique is a structured group meeting that helps resolve differences in group opinion by having individuals generate and then rank a series of ideas in the problem-exploration, alternative-generation, or choice-making stages of the process (Michaelson, Watson, and Black 1989). A group of individuals is presented with a stated problem. Each person individually offers alternative solutions in writing. The group then shares the solutions and lists them on a blackboard or large piece of paper, as in brainstorming. The group discusses and clarifies the ideas. They then rank and vote their preference for the various ideas. If the group has not reached an agreement, it repeats the ranking and voting procedure until the group reaches some agreement.

Nominal group technique encourages innovation, limits conflict, emphasizes equal participation by all members, helps generate consensus, and incorporates the preferences of individuals in decision-making choices. However, unless the administrator is trained in the use of this technique and the ones that follow, it would be more prudent to employ an organizational consultant who is trained and has experience in these techniques to act as a facilitator in the process. Figure 6.2 illustrates the steps in nominal group technique.

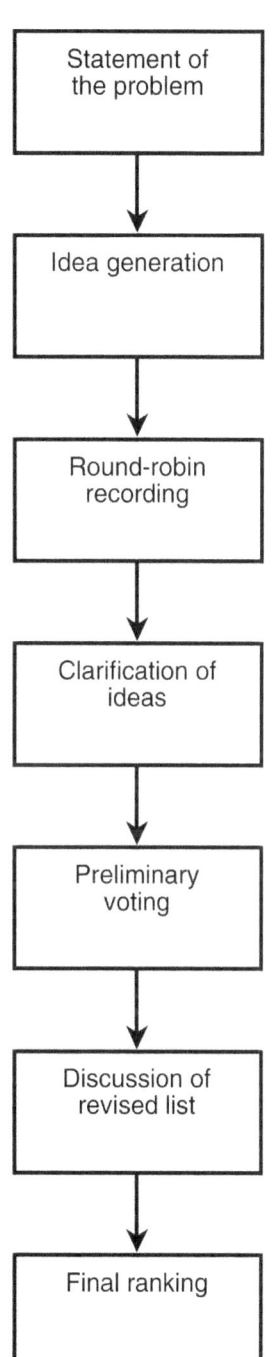

Figure 6.2. Nominal Group Technique

CHAPTER 6

Delphi Technique

Basically, the Delphi technique structures group communication in dealing with a complex problem in four phases: exploration of the subject by individuals, reaching understanding of the group's view of the issues, sharing and evaluation of any reasons for differences, and final evaluation of all information. In the conventional Delphi, a small group designs a questionnaire, which is completed by a larger respondent group; the results are then tabulated and used in developing a revised questionnaire, which is again completed by the larger group. Thus the results of the original polling are fed back to the respondent group to use in subsequent responses. This procedure is repeated until the issues are narrowed, responses are focused, or consensus is reached (Huber 1980).

Delphi is very helpful in a variety of circumstances. First, if the decision makers cannot apply precise analytical techniques to solving the problem but prefer to use subjective judgments on a collective basis, Delphi can provide input from a large number of respondents. Second, if the individuals involved have historically failed to communicate effectively, the Delphi procedures offer a systematic method for ensuring that all opinions are presented. Third, the Delphi does not require face-to-face interaction and thus succeeds when the group is too large for such a direct exchange. Fourth, when time and cost prevent frequent group meetings or when a pre-meeting communication would be helpful, the Delphi technique offers significant value for decision making. Fifth, the Delphi can also overcome situations where individuals greatly disagree or where the anonymity of views must be maintained to protect group members. Finally, the Delphi technique reduces the likelihood of groupthink; it prevents one or more members from dominating by their numbers or the strength of their personality. Figure 6.3 summarizes the steps of the Delphi technique.

CONCLUSION

Decision making is a basic and important process in educational institutions. The success experienced by educational administrators depends largely on their mastery and effective implementation of the decision-making process. In this chapter we described the nature of the decision being made in right-

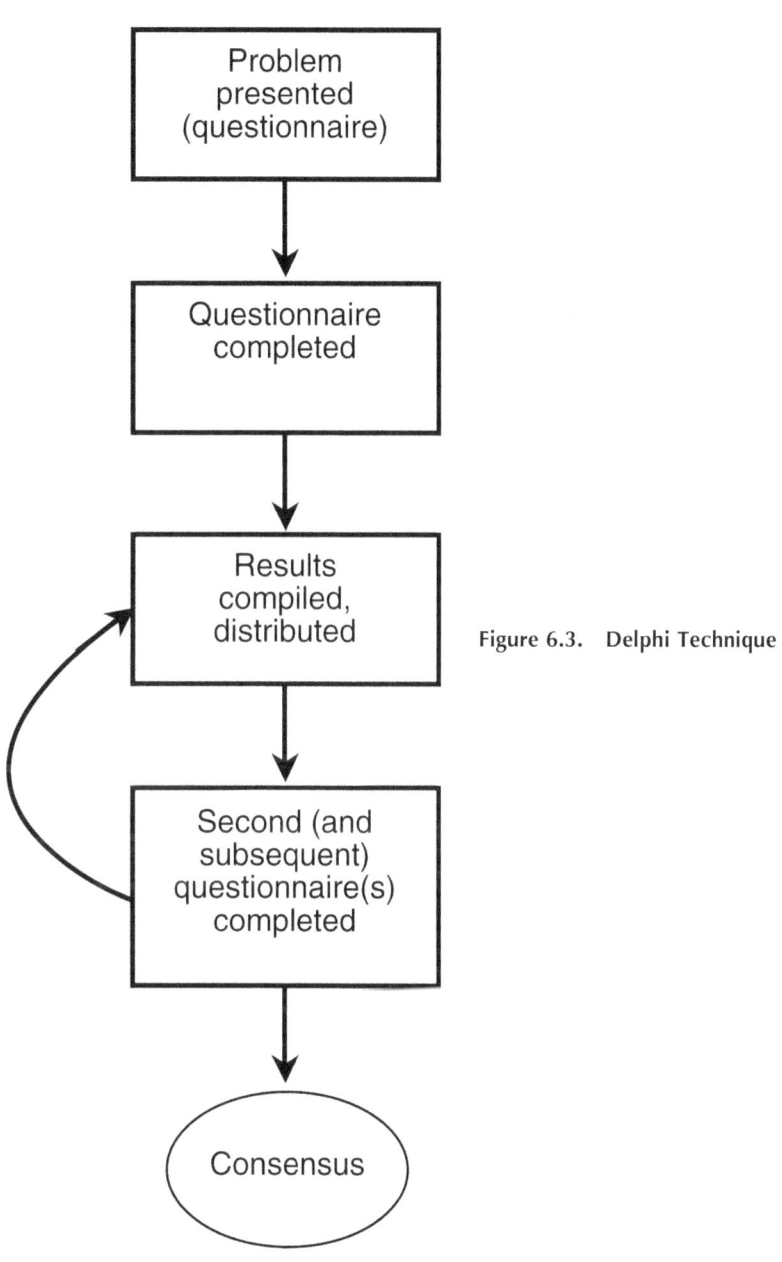

Figure 6.3. Delphi Technique

sizing the Rose Tree School District. We noted that to make such decisions effective, individuals must have technical, interpersonal, and decision-making skills. We outlined basic decision-making processes that help improve the quality of a decision and encourage its acceptance by others. We noted that quality and acceptance are the two most important factors to be considered in making a decision. Decision makers must systematically analyze the situation; set objectives; generate, evaluate, and select alternatives; make the decision; and evaluate the decision made.

In this process we stressed the situational nature of effective decision making. There is no one decision-making style that is effective at all times and in all situations. We concluded by suggesting some techniques to improve decision making, including the nominal group technique, brainstorming, and the Delphi technique. Taking a few minutes each day to determine what decision-making model is best for a given situation is another vital step leading to effective administration.

DIAGNOSTIC CHECKLIST

Here are some questions that may be helpful in assessing the decision-making process in an institution:

- Do organizational members make high-quality, accepted, and ethical decisions?
- Do decision makers follow a rational process of decision making?
- Is the group appropriately involved in decision making?
- Are brainstorming, nominal group technique, the Delphi technique, or other procedures being used to facilitate the decision-making process?

7

ONE-MINUTE ASSESSMENT OF THE CONFLICT MANAGEMENT PROCESS

The adventurer is within us, and he contests for our favour with the social man we are obliged to be. These two sorts of life are incompatible; one we hanker after, the other we are obliged to.

—*William Bolitho*

A few years ago we invited Dr. Janet Baker, a well-known authority on conflict, to address a group of principals at a principal's academy that we were holding at Saint Joseph's University in Philadelphia. We introduced Dr. Baker's topic as "conflict resolution." Upon taking the podium, Dr. Baker quickly corrected us, pointing out that she was there to talk about "conflict management, not conflict resolution." "If your goal as a principal is to resolve all conflict, you will be doomed to frustration and failure," she said. "The best that you can hope for is to *manage* it."

Conflict is the result of incongruent or incompatible relationships between and within individuals, groups, or organizations. Conflict can be public or private, formal or informal, rational or non-rational. The likelihood of conflict increases when parties have the chance to interact, when the parties see their differences as incompatible, and when there is a power differential between the parties that results in the dependence of one party on the other.

CHAPTER 7

Conflict most commonly results in four circumstances. First, when mutually exclusive goals or values actually exist or are perceived to exist by the groups involved, conflict can occur. In the collective bargaining process, for example, the teachers' union may perceive that the administration's goals may be incompatible with those of the teachers, and vice versa. Second, behavior designed to defeat, reduce, or suppress the opponent may cause conflict. Again, union and management have historically experienced conflict for this reason. Third, individuals or groups are dependent on one another. For example, if the second grade teacher does not follow the curriculum, the third grade teacher will be affected because the students will not have been properly prepared. Finally, if each group attempts to create a relatively favored position, conflict may occur. If the English department attempts to show the administration that it is superior to the other departments by demonstrating the others' ineptness, conflict occurs. Knowing these sources of conflict can go a long way toward precluding the surfacing of conflicts in the first place. A little preventative medicine, so to speak, is always in order.

Conflict can have functional or dysfunctional outcomes. Effective administrators learn how to create functional conflict, prevent conflict from arising, and manage dysfunctional conflict when it does occur. They develop and practice techniques for diagnosing the causes and nature of conflict and transforming it into a productive force in the organization. Many colleges, for example, have a healthy competition between and among schools within the university for the recruitment of the most qualified students.

Some conflict is beneficial. It can encourage organizational change in the form of innovation, creativity, and adaption. For example, a number of nonpublic school systems, and even some public school systems, allow schools within the system to compete for the same students. This "open enrollment" policy often spawns innovation in marketing techniques, and more importantly, in curriculum and instruction.

On the other hand, conflict can be viewed as dysfunctional for organizations. It can reduce productivity, decrease morale, cause overwhelming dissatisfaction, and increase tension and stress in the organization. It can arouse anxiety in individuals, increase the tension in an organizational system and its subsystems, and lower satisfaction. Production and satisfaction may decline; turnover and absenteeism may increase.

Administrators have at least five behaviors or strategies for dealing with conflict: avoidance, accommodation, compromise, forcing, and collaboration. Each style is appropriate to different situations that individuals or groups face in organizations. Once again, the underlying theme of contingency theory applies. These behaviors are illustrated in figure 7.1.

AVOIDANCE

Individuals or groups may withdraw from the conflict situation. They act to satisfy neither their own nor the other party's concerns. Avoidance works best when individuals or groups face trivial or tangential issues, when they have little chance of satisfying their personal concerns, when conflict resolution will likely result in significant disruption, or when others can resolve the conflict more effectively. If two secretaries in the secretarial pool, for example, have an argument, the most appropriate strategy for managing the conflict may be avoidance. Let the secretaries resolve the conflict in their own ways. It is like the proverbial story of the next-door neighbors whose children got into an argument and the adults tried to intervene on behalf of their respective children. The adults ended up being lifelong enemies and the children were playing with each other again within the hour.

ACCOMMODATION

Individuals or groups who use accommodation demonstrate willingness to cooperate in satisfying others' concerns, while at the same time acting unassertively in meeting their own. Accommodating individuals often smooth over conflict. This mode builds social capital for later issues, results in harmony and stability, and satisfies others. An assistant principal may capitulate on a disagreement with the principal over a minor matter in hopes that he or she can prevail on a larger issue in the future, thus building political and social capital to be used later. Again, accommodation can be an example of the age-old adage of losing the battle, but winning the war.

Conflict-Handling Modes	Appropriate Situations
Forcing	1. When quick, decisive action is vital—e.g., emergencies. 2. On important issues where unpopular actions need implementing—e.g., cost cutting, enforcing unpopular rules, discipline. 3. On issues vital to the institution's welfare when one is certain that one is right. 4. As a backup when other modes are unsuccessful.
Collaborating	1. To find a win/win solution when both sets of concerns are too important to be compromised. 2. When the objective is to learn. 3. To merge insights from people with different perspectives. 4. To gain commitment by incorporating concerns into a consensus. 5. To work through feelings which have interfered with a relationship.
Compromising	1. When goals are important, but not worth the effort or potential disruption of more assertive modes. 2. When opponents with equal power are committed to mutually exclusive goals. 3. To achieve temporary settlements to complex issues. 4. To arrive at expedient solutions under time pressure. 5. As a backup when collaboration is unsuccessful.
Avoiding	1. When an issue is trivial, or more important issues are pressing. 2. When one perceives no chance of satisfying concerns. 3. When potential disruption outweighs the benefits of resolution. 4. To let people cool down and regain perspective. 5. When the conflicting parties can resolve the conflict more effectively.
Accommodating	1. When one finds one is wrong—to allow a better position to be heard, to learn, and to show one's reasonableness. 2. To build social capital for later use. 3. When harmony and stability are especially important.

Figure 7.1. Conflict Management Styles

COMPROMISE

The compromise mode represents an intermediate behavior. It can include a sharing of positions, but not moving to the extremes. Hence, it often does not maximize satisfaction of both parties. This style works well when goals are important but not sufficiently important for the individual or group to be more assertive, when the two parties have equal power, or when significant time pressure exists. For example, if two grade partners disagree over what supplementary materials should be used for a certain lesson, they may compromise and use some of each teacher's suggestions.

FORCING

Using the forcing mode, one party tries to satisfy its own concerns while showing an unwillingness to satisfy the other's concerns to even a minimal degree. This strategy works well in emergencies, on issues calling for unpopular actions, and in cases where one party is correct in its position or has much greater power. For example, if a child tries to commit suicide, the principal may wish to inform the parents immediately and the guidance counselor may wish it to remain confidential. If the principal arbitrarily informs the parents immediately, he or she is using forcing behavior.

COLLABORATION

The collaboration mode emphasizes problem solving with a goal of maximizing satisfaction for both parties, often resulting in a win/win solution. It means seeing conflict as natural, showing trust and honesty toward others, and encouraging the airing of every person's attitudes and feelings. Each party exerts both assertive and cooperative behavior. Parties can use it when their objectives are to learn, to use information from diverse sources, and to find an integrative solution. If the teacher's union and the school board agree to consider their differences to be "our" problems rather than "your" problems, they are taking a collaborative or problem-solving approach to resolve or avoid conflict.

A rule of thumb that I have found effective is, once one decides that avoidance is not appropriate, to begin efforts toward conflict resolution with the collaborative mode. If that is not successful, move progressively to compromise and accommodation, using forcing only as a last resort.

DIAGNOSTIC CHECKLIST

Here are some questions that may help you assess the conflict management capabilities of your institution:

- Is the conflict in the institution functional or dysfunctional?
- Are preventative measures being employed to preclude conflict from occurring?
- Are there mechanisms for effectively managing conflict and stress?
- Does the use of these mechanisms reflect the situational nature of conflict resolution?
- Are avoidance, compromise, forcing, accommodation, and collaboration utilized in the appropriate situations?

8

ONE-MINUTE ASSESSMENT OF THE DISTRIBUTION OF POWER

The power of a man is his present means to obtain some future apparent good.

—*Thomas Hobbes*

Charlotte Burton is the new principal of Springfield High School. She met Marie Wilson, the teacher union representative, on her first day at the school. The two women are both strong-willed individuals who reached their respective positions by aggressively pursuing their professional goals. They are both intent on showing the other who is "boss."

The scenario here is not unlike many that occur at educational institutions of all levels. This situation reflects the exercise of power in an organization. Power is the potential or actual ability to influence others in a desired direction. An individual, group, or other social unit has power if it controls information, knowledge, or resources desired by another individual, group, or social unit. Who has the power in the situation described at Springfield High School? At Springfield High School, both Charlotte Burton and Marie Wilson have power. How well each one uses her power and negotiation skills will determine her effectiveness.

CHAPTER 8

In this chapter, we examine power and the negotiations process. We begin by considering the reasons individuals or groups exert power. We then examine the sources from which they derive power. Next, we examine the collective bargaining process. We describe two bargaining paradigms, the negotiation process, and some of the strategies and tactics used in negotiations.

POWER IN THE ORGANIZATION

Organizational researchers have increasingly cited the value of identifying and using power behavior to improve individual and organizational performance, even calling its development and use "the central executive function" (Kotter 1977). Theorists and practitioners have transformed an early view of power, which considered it evil and primarily stemming from coercion, into a model of viable political action in organizations. Yet, although functional and advantageous in many situations, power behavior can also create conflict, which frequently is dysfunctional for the organization (Kaplan 1964).

ETHICAL ISSUES

How legitimate is the use of power in organizations? Certainly, if the use of power is manipulative and autocratic, it raises questions about the ethics of power. The abuse of power is evident not only in politics, but also in schools, school districts, and institutions of higher education.

Administrators should establish guidelines for the ethical use of power in their institutions. They and other organizational members must emphasize power's contribution to organizational effectiveness and control its abuses. Ensuring that the rights of all organizational members are guaranteed is one criterion for its ethical use. This is especially appropriate in institutions that are not unionized, where the faculty and staff handbook should outline employee rights in a way similar to that of a labor agreement. In chapter 11 we speak of developing covenants or informal agreements between employees and management.

ASSESSMENT OF THE DISTRIBUTION OF POWER

POWER AND DEPENDENCE

We can initially diagnose the level of power someone has by estimating the extent of the dependence that flows in the opposite direction from power in a relationship (Kotter 1977). In other words, the power that Charlotte Burton has over Marie Wilson is determined by the degree of dependence that Marie Wilson has on Charlotte Burton.

Dependence arises in part because a person, group, or organization relies on another person, group, or organization to accomplish his, her, or its tasks. A subordinate depends on his or her ordinates for assistance in accomplishing a task and identifying obstacles to achieving a work goal. The person being relied or depended upon automatically has some power to influence the other.

Marie Wilson, for example, might attempt to have the untenured teachers believe that their continued employment depends largely on her support as a way to increase their dependence on her. On the other hand, Charlotte Burton might circumvent Marie Wilson as much as possible to display her independence from union influence and demonstrate to the teachers that their future employment depends more on Charlotte Burton than on Marie Wilson.

EMPOWERING OTHERS

In site-based or school-based management situations, for example, superintendents and principals are relinquishing some of their power. Task forces, whose membership reflects the makeup of the school community, are given either advisory or governance power in making decisions. This process empowers faculty and staff, but ultimately enhances the power of the administration, because the school is more likely to achieve its goals. If it does, the administration looks good, which, in effect, increases its power.

SOURCES OF POWER

There are at least three sources of power in an organization: position power, personal power, and information or resource power.

CHAPTER 8

Possessing position power, administrators can exert influence over others simply because of the authority associated with their jobs. It results in subordinates obeying the instructions given by a principal, for example, simply by virtue of the position that he or she holds. In education, the union contract and tenure mitigate the principal's position power to a significant degree. Thus, it is inappropriate to rely on position as the only source of power. One study showed, for example, that as a supervisor's position power increased, a subordinate's compliance increased, but his or her satisfaction with supervision decreased (Rahim 1989). So, in the long run, the abuse of position power can have diminishing returns.

Power accrues to other positions because of their centrality. The more the activities of a position are linked and important to those of other individuals or subunits, the greater its centrality. A superintendent of schools, for example, has greater centrality than the school board because the activities of more jobs are linked to him or her than to the elected school board. Thus, even though the school board technically has more position power, in reality, the superintendent has more power because of the centrality of his or her position.

Personal Power

Personal power is based on the knowledge or personality of an individual that allows him or her to influence the behavior of others. An individual who has unique or special knowledge, skills, or experience can use this expertise as a source of influence and as a way of building personal power. When the use of computers first made its impact on schools, for example, the "computer guru" on the faculty oftentimes wielded personal power based on his or her special knowledge and skills. As schools and other organizations have become increasingly technology oriented, technical support staff have acquired increased power.

Some individuals influence others because they have charisma or because others identify with them. An individual with charisma often exerts power because he or she attracts others to follow. Oftentimes, when lateral dependence occurs among peers, it is the result of personal power based on the individual's charisma.

Resource Power

Access to resources or information provides a third major source of influence. This differs from expert power in its greater transience. Expertise is more permanent than information-based power. For example, the first individuals to learn to use a new computer system might initially derive their power from having information that others do not, but if their power persists even after the average teacher becomes computer literate, he or she has developed personal power based on expertise.

Power can come from the control of scarce resources, such as money, materials, staff, or information. In a school setting, the business manager oftentimes has this type of power. Even the audiovisual director can have this type of power if there is a greater demand than there is a supply of these types of resources in a school.

THE NEGOTIATIONS PROCESS

In the field of education, perhaps the prototypical display of power occurs through the negotiations or collective bargaining process. Negotiation is a process by which two or more parties attempt to reach an agreement that is acceptable to all parties about issues on which they disagree. Negotiations typically have four key elements (Lax and Sebenius 1986). First, the two parties demonstrate some degree of interdependence. Charlotte Burton and Marie Wilson demonstrate such interdependence. Second, some perceived conflict exists between the parties involved in the negotiations. Ordinarily, the teachers' union and the school administration differ in their views on exactly how the school should operate. Third, the two parties have the potential to participate in opportunistic interaction. Therefore, each party tries to influence the other through various negotiating actions. Each party cares about and pursues its own interests, by trying to influence decisions to its advantage. Finally, the possibility of agreement or settlement exists.

CHAPTER 8

BARGAINING PARADIGMS

Basically, two bargaining paradigms are in current use, distributive bargaining, which takes an adversarial or win-lose approach, and integrative bargaining, which takes a problem-solving or win-win approach.

The classical view considers bargaining as a win-lose situation, where one party's gain is the other party's loss. Known also as a zero-sum type of negotiation, because the gain of one party equals the loss of the other and hence the net is zero, this approach characterizes the great majority of the negotiations taking place in educational settings today.

Recent research encourages negotiators to transform the bargaining into a win-win situation. Here, both parties gain as a result of the negotiations. Known also as a positive-sum type of negotiation, because the gains of each party yield a positive sum, this approach has recently characterized the negotiations in a few school districts, especially those that have had a history of strikes and are looking for an alternative to the classical model of collective bargaining.

Integrative/Collaborative Bargaining

Even when an agreement is reached, distributive bargaining tends to lead to a win-lose conclusion between the parties. Both parties tend to depict the other as the loser to their respective constituencies. When the negotiations break down into a serious impasse, the probability of a lose/lose outcome increases. In this circumstance, not only are the parties frustrated from achieving a satisfactory agreement, but those whom they serve are affected adversely. The teaching-learning environment can be disrupted by the hostility between the parties. Parents, students, and the community in general can become angry when the school is unable to function properly because of unsettled disputes between the school's management and its employees (Fisher and Ury 1981).

An alternative form of bargaining has emerged as a way to avoid or minimize the negative aspects of adversarial bargaining. Collaborative bargaining represents a cooperative process that focuses on problem solving and other activities that identify, enlarge, and act upon the common interests of the parties. Its objective is to increase the joint gain of the parties, the win-win outcome.

The pressure for educational reform in the last two decades has stimulated teachers and school boards to negotiate collaboratively over policy issues dealing with class size, staff development, student achievement on standardized tests, and teacher appraisal methods. Collaborative bargaining is a timely method for joining the general trend of school reforms that seek to institutionalize collaborative decision making into the daily operations of schools. Collaborative bargaining rests on the assumptions that both parties want to achieve a mutually satisfactory agreement and that the agreement will lead to an improved school environment for students.

An example of an integrative or collaborative bargaining approach is the win-win process developed by Irving Goldaber. In this process, the parties are given a fixed period of time in which to negotiate a contract. In so doing, the parties are to arrive at shared solutions without being forced to give up their desired goals (Palestini 2011).

Goldaber's win-win approach is organized into ten phases depicted in table 8.1. The preliminary phases entail each party receiving the protocols for structuring the process and preparing lists of questions, concerns, and expectations. These lists are copied onto large sheets of paper for posting around the room during the first formal meeting of the process.

Table 8.1. Goldaber's Win-Win Contract Development Program

Phase	Activity
1	Both sides receive protocols governing the process.
2	Each side lists questions and concerns for Phase 3
	Weekend 1: The Communications Laboratory
3	All participants and the facilitator meet.
4	Issues are identified for inclusion in the contract and contract matter committees are appointed.
5	Committees discuss issues, finalize agreements, and list unresolved issues (approximately thirty days allowed).
	Weekend 2
6	All participants and the facilitator meet to reach agreement on the contract.
7	The writing committee writes the proposed contract.
8	All participants review the proposed contract and recommend its approval to their constituencies.
9	Each side votes on the proposed contract.
10	All participants meet to witness the signing of the contract.

The third and fourth phases occur during the first two weekends that bound the fixed time period (usually thirty days) for reaching an agreement. This weekend is conducted as a communications laboratory to deal with areas of distrust and to reach the realization that each side needs the other to resolve its conflicts. The questions prepared in phase two provide a way for the parties to communicate and share their concerns with each other.

The laboratory usually begins on a Friday evening and extends through all day Saturday. The participants are representatives of the two parties (an equal number from both sides, plus resource persons they invite) and an external facilitator who conducts the laboratory. The end goal of the laboratory, the fourth phase, is to identify issues for collective bargaining and to appoint contract matter committees.

During the next thirty days, the fifth phase, the contract matter committees meet, discuss, and attempt to reach agreement on issues to be included in a collective bargaining agreement. One committee might address salary and benefits; a second, working conditions; and a third, rights and responsibilities. A fourth committee might be established to deal with any items not assigned to the other committees. Its job is to finalize agreement on as many items as possible. Unresolved issues are to be listed and brought to the second weekend meeting of the entire group.

Collective bargaining itself takes place during the committee meetings. But rather than following the traditional distributive approach, the parties are urged to seek new and creative solutions to problems. They are also encouraged to concede voluntarily on positions whenever it is possible to do so. Mutual respect and empathy for the greater good of the school should guide the deliberations.

At the end of the fixed period for bargaining, all participants reconvene for a second weekend (phase six). Agreed-upon items are confirmed, and unresolved items are addressed. When success is achieved in reaching agreement on all items, a contract-writing committee is appointed to put the agreement in final form. The remaining phases, seven through ten, deal with reviewing and recommending the proposed agreement, formal ratification, and the signing of the contract.

The use of the Goldaber model has been more successful in affecting attitudes than the content of the agreements. The model has had an astounding success rate, with management and employees citing a freer, more open exchange and a problem-solving approach that promoted greater awareness of the other side's point of view on issues. One of the drawbacks to the process, however, is that both management and employee constituencies may be locked into the distributive paradigm of negotiations. There is a tendency to think that the best possible agreement has not been achieved because negotiations do not necessarily continue until Labor Day. In order for the process to be effective, then, a great deal of staff development needs to take place before negotiations even begin so that both parties' constituencies have realistic expectations of what the results of the process will be.

EFFECTIVE NEGOTIATIONS

We can identify at least four basic steps in effective negotiation for either distributive or integrative bargaining. First, the parties prepare for the negotiations. Second, they determine the model they will use and develop their bargaining strategies. Third, they negotiate a settlement, and fourth, they administer the agreed-upon contract (Goldaber 1987).

Pre-negotiation Preparation

The preparation phase of the negotiation process is as important as the negotiations themselves. It is with proper preparation that many problems during the actual negotiations can be precluded. The preparation phase begins the day after the last contract is signed. It continues until the next contract is negotiated, but picks up in intensity about six months before the negotiation sessions begin. One of the first steps in the preparation process is to anticipate the issues that will be negotiated. An effective way of doing this is to review the grievances that have occurred during the administration of the current contract. This review will identify the problematic areas of the present contract and be an accurate indicator of what will most likely be the substance of the upcoming negotiations.

Another step in the preparation process is the gathering of information regarding comparable settlements in other school districts and institutions similar to your own. Data regarding the Consumer Price Index is also important to have. Demographic data regarding the school district, like the average age of the faculty, student enrollment projections, property tax expectations, and budget projections, should be gathered. Finally, the negotiation team should be assembled during this phase.

The makeup of the negotiation team should reflect appropriate segments of the school community. From management's point of view, the team should include representatives from the central office, local school administrators, and a member of the school board. Many times, legal counsel is part of the team and frequently serves as the chief negotiator. It is not advisable for the superintendent or the highest-ranking administrative officer to be on the team because that person needs to remain the respected leader of the school district after the contract is negotiated and should not be associated too closely with what is too often an adversarial process.

The choice of chief negotiator is the next step in constituting the negotiating team. This person must be knowledgeable of the prevailing collective bargaining laws and the bargaining process itself. The abilities to plan, analyze, and coordinate the activities of the team are essential. Being able to articulate the various positions is also extremely important. The personal qualities of tolerance and persistence are needed to ensure that the process is conducted in a rational, calm manner and is kept on course toward achieving an agreement.

From a practical perspective, team members should be identified according to the expertise needed in the process. One person, generally the chief negotiator, should be a skilled spokesperson. Another member should be a specialist in the wording of proposals; another in cost analysis; another in keeping written records of key discussions; and at least one who knows the current contract provisions thoroughly.

Developing a Bargaining Strategy

The second phase of the negotiation process is developing the bargaining strategy. This phase includes the mutual decision of whether a distributive or an integrated model is to be used. Once a model is selected, the identification of key issues takes place. Management must determine what goals it plans to achieve as a result of the process. For example, management might wish to hold the line on school governance issues or on salary and fringe benefit costs to 1 percent above the cost-of-living increase.

Management might wish to rectify a salary inequity between junior and senior faculty or address a class-size issue. Once the broad-based goals are developed, a rationale for each proposal needs to be prepared (Fisher and Brown 1988).

The Bargaining Process

Maintaining an atmosphere of reasonableness and civility during the bargaining process is important if a settlement is to be reached. Certain protocols should be maintained so that common courtesy prevails. Once the proper atmosphere is established, the negotiators can go about their business of presenting, evaluating, and responding to each other's proposals. Once proposals are presented, those that have cost implications need to be identified and "costed out." It is an effective tactic to consider the cost items as a "package," rather than individually.

It is essential that the negotiation team presents a united front. Never disagree on an issue at the bargaining table. If there is disagreement or misunderstanding among members of the team, a private caucus should be called to resolve the differences before returning to the table. In addition, a careful rationale for each proposal should be developed and a reasoned response to the other parties' proposals should be articulated. It is also effective to accept certain of the other parties' proposals as a "trade-off" for the acceptance of one of your own proposals. Finally, when reaching agreement on an issue, be certain that the proper wording is incorporated into the contract because the parties will have to live with it for the duration of the agreement.

When the parties fail to reach a settlement, an impasse may be declared. In the case of many educational institutions, state law determines how an impasse is handled. In general, however, the process may proceed from mediation to fact finding and then to arbitration.

The mediation process is one through which a third party seeks to facilitate the process and resolve the impasse. The objective is to assist the parties to arrive at an agreement of their own creation. The mediator typically meets with each party's negotiating team separately to explain the process and to ascertain each party's view of the disputed issues. Then, in a joint meeting, the mediator summarizes the issues with the effort to ensure that each party's position is understood clearly by the other. After further meetings with each team, the mediator develops a proposed settlement for presentation to both parties that will end the impasse.

The fact-finding process leads to a set of independently developed recommendations for a settlement of the impasse. Prior to fact finding, the parties prepare their cases with supporting documentation and arguments. The fact-finder considers the cases and develops a report. The fact-finder's report may be accepted or rejected by one or both parties. If the report is made public, it may be persuasive in the parties' eventual acceptance.

If neither mediation nor fact finding is effective in resolving an impasse, binding arbitration is often the result. The arbitration can be voluntary or mandatory, advisory or binding. However, if mediation and/or fact finding has not been successful, binding arbitration is the only viable solution short of a strike.

In arbitration, the parties usually have the right to select or reject names from a list of potential arbitrators. The selected arbitrator conducts a hearing at which each party presents its written exhibits and oral testimony. Within a reasonable period after the hearing, the arbitrator's decision is issued. If binding arbitration is used, the decision resolves the impasse and the arbitrator's report becomes the "settlement."

Contract Administration

A successful collective bargaining process leads to an agreement or contract that determines the conditions of employment for its duration. If an educational administrator is to be an effective and respected leader in the school community, it is essential that he or she "know the contract." Failing to do so will lead to embarrassing contract breeches that will undermine the administrator's competence and any culture of trust that has been established. Thus, principals and other administrators should participate in training sessions about the newly adopted contract. Preparation of an administrator's manual, which includes interpretation of contract clauses, procedures for processing grievances, and contractual deadlines, should take place.

SUMMARY

Power might be one of the least understood, but most important areas of educational administration. This chapter described the sources and uses of

ASSESSMENT OF THE DISTRIBUTION OF POWER

power in institutions. We identified position power, personal power, and resource- and information-based power.

We continued by looking at negotiation as the ritualized use of power in organizations. Two bargaining paradigms, distributive and integrative, were described and compared. Then, the process of negotiation was outlined; the steps include preparation, model selection and strategy development, negotiating an agreement, and contract administration.

It is likely that most educational administrators will not be integrally involved in the bargaining process because that duty is usually assigned to a collective bargaining specialist. However, all educational administrators will be responsible for the administration of the contract and ultimately be involved in contract grievances. It is important, therefore, to know the process whereby the contract was established and to know the nuances of its implementation. Many an administrator has been rendered ineffective, and has even been considered incompetent, because of an insufficient knowledge of the details and implications of the labor agreement. Thus, a thorough understanding of the document and a humane implementation of it are essential elements to an educational administrator's eventual success.

DIAGNOSTIC CHECKLIST

Here are some questions that may be helpful in assessing the distribution of power in an institution:

- Is power appropriately shared?
- What type of negotiations occur in the school district or higher education institution?
- Do the negotiations tend to be distributive or integrative?
- What degree of preparation takes place?
- Is the contract language understood by the administrators?
- Are provisions made for the proper administration of the contract?

9

ONE-MINUTE ASSESSMENT OF THE STRATEGIC PLANNING PROCESS

Planning is all, but plans are nothing.

—*Dwight D. Eisenhower*

Blanchard and Johnson posit that the effective manager must spend time developing goals and placing them in the context of a vision. There is much to be said as to the wisdom of this assertion, especially in educational settings. There is a plethora of scholarly school research that corroborates their recommendation. A number of studies have found that when schools develop clear and agreed-upon goals that are duly promulgated, such schools are usually effective. Thus effective educational administrators need to develop an educational vision that is mutually acceptable and understood by all components of the school community.

In some circles exactly what constitutes an educational vision seems to be shrouded in mystery. Actually, the process of developing an educational vision is not all that complex. The first step is to identify a list of broad goals. This step in the process should be done in conjunction with representatives from all components of the school community. Otherwise, there will be no sense of "ownership" on the part of the school community, which will jeopardize the successful implementation of the vision and its goals. "All children achieving" is an example of such a broad goal.

CHAPTER 9

The next step in the process is to merge and prioritize the goals, and summarize them in the form of a short and concise statement. The following is an example of a vision statement:

> Our vision for the Exeter School System is that all of our graduating students, regardless of ability, will say that "I have received an excellent education that has prepared me to be an informed citizen and leader in my community." In addition, our students will be committed to a process of lifelong learning and the making of a better world by living the ideals of fairness and justice and service to others.

The key concepts in the above vision statement are "all students can learn," "academic excellence," "leadership," "lifelong learning," "values," and community "service." These are the concepts or goals that the ten-minute educational leader needs to stress in all forms of communication and in all of his or her interpersonal relations with the various members of the school community.

The final step in the process is the "institutionalizing" of the vision. This step ensures that the vision endures even when the leadership in the institution changes. Operationalizing and placing the important concepts of the vision into the official policies and procedures of the school system is one important way of helping to institutionalize the educational vision and incorporate it into the school culture. Figures 9.1a and 9.1b depict a typical institutional mission and the objectives, parameters, and strategies that flow from it.

Another way of institutionalizing a vision is by encouraging the development of "heroes" who embody the institution's vision and "tribal storytellers," who promulgate it (Palestini 2012). We have often heard individuals in various organizations describe a colleague as "an institution around here." Heroes such as these do more to establish the organizational culture of an institution than any manual or policies and procedures handbook ever could. The senior faculty member who is recognized and respected for his or her knowledge of the subject matter as well as his or her humane treatment of students is an invaluable asset to an educational institution. He or she is a symbol of what the institution stands for. It is the presence of these heroes that sustains the reputation of the institution and allows the workforce to feel good about itself and about where it works. The deeds and accomplish-

> **Beliefs**
> Statements of the schools' and community's fundamental convictions, values, and character.
> We believe that:
> - The family provides the foundation for the development of the individual.
> - The family, community, and school share the responsibility for education, and the student is ultimately responsible for learning.
> - Expectation influences achievement.
> - Education is vital to a strong, healthy community.
> - A safe, positive learning environment is crucial to education.
> - Quality education empowers an individual to achieve potential.
> - Learning builds self esteem and self esteem promotes learning.
> - Learning is a life-long process.
> - The ability to accept and direct change is vital to continued growth.
> - Each individual has dignity and worth.
> - Ethical behavior is necessary for a just society.
> - All students can learn.
> - Students learn at different rates and in different ways.
> - The commitment of every person within the organization is essential to its success.
>
> **Mission**
> The mission of the Fredericksburg Area School District, in partnership with families and community, is to provide each student with a foundation for life-long learning, to ensure all students are responsible contributors in a rapidly changing society, and to support community needs by providing dynamic leadership, excellent teaching, and diverse, innovative programs.
>
> **Objectives**
> To graduate 100% of our students
> To give each graduate the knowledge, skills, and attitudes necessary for lifelong learning
> To challenge all students to acquire the knowledge and skills necessary to achieve their potential and to pursue their aspirations
> To have each student volunteer to provide community service

Figures 9.1a. Strategic Planning Example

ments of these heroes need to be promulgated and need to become part of the folklore of the institution.

The deeds of these heroes are usually perpetuated by the "tribal storytellers" in an organization. These are the individuals who know the history of the organization and relate it through stories of its former and present heroes. An effective leader encourages the tribal storytellers, knowing that they are serving an invaluable service in an institution. They work at the process of institutional renewal. They allow the institution to continuously improve. They preserve and revitalize the values of the institution. They mitigate the tendency of institutions, especially educational institutions, to

> **Parameters**
> 1. We will practice participative management at all levels of the organization.
> 2. No new program or service will be accepted unless
>   - it is consistent with the Strategic Plan
>   - anticipated benefits clearly justify costs
>   - provisions are made for staff development and program evaluation
> 1. No program or service will be retained unless benefits justify costs and it continues to make a positive contribution to the mission.
> 2. Nothing will take precedence over the K-12 instructional program.
> 3. We will not tolerate behavior that demeans the dignity or the self-worth of any student, staff, or community member.
>
> **Strategies**
> 1. We will foster a climate of trust and cooperation through open communication and participation.
> 2. We will provide a nonthreatening, caring, disciplined learning environment where mutual respect exists.
> 3. Using our curriculum as a base, we will identify the outcomes essential for lifelong learning and develop means to assess whether students achieve them.
> 4. We will energize and integrate all aspects of our diverse community to address the social and emotional needs of our students, which interfere with learning.
> 5. We will work in partnership with students, parents, and community to establish a volunteer service program to teach all students, at all levels, the value of community service.
> 6. We will develop and implement plans to set challenging and appropriate expectations for every student (student expectations, parent expectations, and staff expectations).
> 7. We will examine alternative methods of financing and managing revenue and resources.
> 8. We will identify and implement a variety of effective instructional techniques and support services, so that 100% of our students graduate, have the knowledge and skills required for lifelong learning, and realize their potential.

Figures 9.1b.   Strategic Planning Example

become bureaucratic. Every institution has heroes and storytellers. It is the educational leader's job to see to it that things like manuals and handbooks don't replace them.

A STRATEGIC PLANNING PROCESS FOR EDUCATIONAL INSTITUTIONS

Ten specifically identified activities would be included in a strategic plan for academic planning in educational institutions. They include the following:

ASSESSMENT OF THE STRATEGIC PLANNING PROCESS

1. Develop a Mission Statement. The process of developing a mission statement involves establishing a strong group consensus about the unique purposes of the educational institution and its place in the community that it serves. The process of development of the mission will set the tone for all further planning activity. Most often, educational institutions have an existing mission. However, the planning process should not begin until there is broad acceptance of the current mission. Many times, the mission needs to be revised to adapt to current circumstances before the process can continue.

    The educational vision of the school is derived from the mission statement. It is often a concise summary of the mission or how you expect your mission to play out for the future.

2. Develop a Set of Institutional Goals. The institution should next develop a set of goals that it deems appropriate in the accomplishment of its mission. Goals are more specific and give direction to the action that needs to take place to achieve them. The goals should be expressed in terms that would promote easy assessment. It should be clear to an objective observer whether they have been achieved. An example of a goal that would be derived from the mission statement listed earlier would be "to provide an education that addresses all dimensions of a student's character—mental, psychological, physical, and spiritual."

3. Develop Learning Outcomes Statements. The process of developing student learning outcomes statements, including transitional outcomes, should include the outcomes students must achieve in order to meet the institutional goals and progress from one level to the next. For example, from the primary to the intermediate level, intermediate level to middle level, and middle level to the high school program. An example of a typical outcome statement might be "upon completing the American history course, the student will have the ability to research a topic in history, analyze its causes and effects, and determine its implications for the future."

    Ways of authentically assessing these educational outcomes also need to be developed. The current emphasis on outcomes-based education (OBE), authentic assessment, and portfolio assessment focuses quite heavily on this step in the planning process.

4. Determine Graduation Requirements. The logical next step to developing outcome statements is to establish a set of criteria that will be used to determine achievement of student learning outcomes that will be required for graduation. In other words, the number and the degree to which the outcomes must be mastered in order to receive the culminating credential of the institution.
5. Develop the Curriculum. The essence of the conversion from a class time–based system to a student learning outcomes–based system is the revision of all academic courses to reflect student learning outcome statements. The courses should be developed to include a number of the learning outcomes determined earlier. Courses should be developed until all of the learning outcomes have been incorporated into at least one of the courses.
6. Conduct a Comprehensive Needs Analysis. The needs analysis is a crucial part of the strategic planning process. It must involve a comprehensive identification of both internal and external strengths and weaknesses and include an analysis of instructional practices. The process should rely on quantitative data whenever possible. It should involve all "stakeholder" groups within the local community, giving each an opportunity to provide both hard data and informed opinion. The result of the needs analysis should be the main tool in developing priority goal areas for action planning.
7. Develop a List of Priorities. Priorities are identified by a process that applies the information accumulated during the needs analysis to the list of general institutional goals identified earlier. Those goals that show need for developmental action are prioritized on the basis of their relationship to the identified mission and on the severity of the need. One or more action plans or strategies are developed for each of the priorities.
8. Develop Specific Action Plans. One or more action plans or strategies are to be developed for each of the priority goal areas. The action plans are to identify specific actions to be taken to meet the identified priority needs. Action plans should include:
   a. Objectives;
   b. Major strategies to be completed;
   c. Projected time lines or completion dates;

d. The person or group responsible;
   e. Estimated costs, if any;
   f. Evaluation or assessment questions.
9. Develop an Assessment Plan. The assessment plan ascertains the degree to which the student learning outcomes are achieved. The assessment plan should include the following:
   a. The general purpose of the assessments;
   b. A description of the process to be used to develop and analyze portfolios of student work, including a variety of strategies;
   c. A description of assessment procedures to be used;
   d. A description of how the assessment results will be used;
   e. A description of how the school will assist students who have not demonstrated mastery of the outcomes;
   f. A description of the process for notifying the public of assessment results.
10. Prepare a Professional Development Plan. The final step in the academic planning process is to prepare a professional development plan to train and prepare the staff to implement the plans. This step is especially important if new and innovative approaches are required to implement the strategic plan.

DIAGNOSTIC CHECKLIST

Here are a few questions that you can address in assessing your institution's understanding and commitment to its goals:

- Does a mission statement exist?
- Does a vision statement exist?
- Does a strategic plan exist?
- Are the goals, objectives, and strategies clear and measurable?
- Are they known and understood by the school community?
- Is the planning process ongoing?

10

ONE-MINUTE ASSESSMENT OF THE TOLERANCE FOR CHANGE

To live is to change, and to be perfect is to have changed often.

—*John Henry Newman*

Changing an educational institution or system has been described as making a U-turn with the *Queen Elizabeth 2*. In some cases, resistance to change is so extreme that the cruise ship metaphor can be considered an understatement. Despite its difficulty, the process of change is absolutely necessary if an organization is to continually improve. Thus, to be an effective leader, especially in the transformational style, an administrator must become a change agent and master the process that can bring change about effectively.

AN INTEGRATED APPROACH TO CHANGE

The literature is replete with various suggested change processes. Many of them contain elements that are helpful in leading to successful transformation, but few contain all of the necessary elements. As a result, through the process of trial and error, I have developed my own process for change. I call it an integrated change process because although there are distinct steps in the process, the key to their successful implementation is that many of them are implemented simultaneously rather than sequentially.

In an earlier work, entitled *Ten Steps to Educational Reform: Making Change Happen*, I suggest the following steps in the process (Palestini 2004):

- Establishing a climate for change
- Assessing the need for change
- Creating a sense of urgency
- Assessing favorable and opposing forces
- Selecting among alternatives
- Promoting ownership
- Providing professional development
- Operationalizing the change
- Evaluating the change
- Institutionalizing the change

Most attempts at effecting change in the form of educational reform fail because leaders have no formal plan at all or do not engage in all the steps in the process. Other failures occur when administrators try to implement the reform by following the change process steps sequentially rather than simultaneously and get bogged down in one or another of the steps, unable to bring the process to closure.

Whether it be an apparently insignificant change, such as deciding between the homogenous or the heterogeneous grouping of students (tracking), or what form of assessment should be used in college admission, or a more significant reform, such as whether tuition vouchers should be used to restructure and reform public education, I am suggesting that the implementation of these steps in an integrated way will successfully bring about the desired change.

Establishing a Climate for Change

E. Mark Hanson, in his text entitled *Educational Administration and Organizational Behavior*, describes an incident regarding the process of change.

Always interested in the processes of school improvement, he once asked the superintendent of a large, urban school district, "How does change come about around here?" She thought for a moment. "Well," she replied, "there is the normal way and the miraculous way. The normal way," she continued, "is where the heavens part and the angels come down and do the change for us. The miraculous way is when we do it ourselves" (Hanson 1991).

If one has established a climate of change at his or her institution, change will come to be expected. It will be perceived as something positive and routine. The need for change in the context of continuous improvement should be articulated constantly by institutional leaders. College presidents, superintendents, and principals should set the tone for change by taking every opportunity to articulate its necessity and model it in their own leadership. For example, the faculty convocations can be occasions for articulating the notion that if the institution is to progress, academically and operationally, it must be open to change. At the initial meeting, the possible changes that are anticipated during the upcoming academic year can be shared. At subsequent faculty meetings, the need for change can be reinforced.

In addition to articulating the need for change, to promote a positive school climate the leader must model a tolerance for change. Even in something as simple as changing the color of the school lockers every two or three years or changing the format of faculty meetings to incorporate innovative concepts like cooperative learning and shared decision making, the leader needs to lead by example. The leader must be perceived as being open to new ideas and providing a climate in which creativity is fostered. In other words, we must "be the change that we expect in others."

If a positive climate for change is to be established, another requisite is an environment of trust and respect. Institutions do not amount to anything without the people who make them what they are. The individuals most influential in making institutions what they are, are essentially volunteers. Our very best teachers and administrators can work anywhere they please. So, in a sense, they volunteer to work where they do. As educational leaders, we would do far better if we looked on and treated our salaried employees with the deference with which we treat volunteers.

CHAPTER 10

Assessing a Need

The next step in the integrated change process is the needs assessment. Unfortunately, this step is often ignored. Many educational leaders become enamored with one educational reform or another and try to implement it whether or not there is an identified and agreed-upon need. Reforms, such as the whole language approach to reading, cooperative learning, block scheduling, interdisciplinary curricula, distance learning, and even site-based management, have been adopted arbitrarily by misguided educational administrators. When implemented without a needs assessment these changes are almost always destined to fail.

Ordinarily, a needs assessment calls for a review of existing data and may require some surveying of the various components or stakeholders of the school community. There is always a certain risk in a needs assessment. In the process of uncovering needs, one might also raise expectations that all of the respondent's concerns will be addressed. Fundamental to effecting change is priority setting and focus; thus, not all needs can be met immediately. Resources are in short supply, and difficult; sometimes painful decisions have to be made about which from an array of crucial needs requires attention. Three reference groups are especially important to the needs assessment and the change process: students and parents, professional staff, and educational policy makers. Oftentimes, it is the students and/or parents who are left out of the process. Leaving them out, of course, has distribution of power and motivation implications and empirical research suggests that inclusion is much preferred to exclusion.

Data about students are readily available in the records a typical educational institution generates and maintains. Standardized test scores, attendance records, free or reduced-price lunch recipients, percentage of students with disabilities, transportation reports, and a host of other official and unofficial data serve as sources for developing a profile of the students in the school or school district. Informal discussions with colleagues, other professionals, and the students and parents themselves are another source of information. Student focus groups and systematic observation by both teachers and administrators are still other ways of assessing whether there is a need for change in the school.

Central office personnel, local and state board members, state departments of education, legislators, the United States Department of Education, and education advocacy groups should also be consulted to identify the needs of the educational institution. Lastly, the reports of accrediting agencies, such as the Middle States Association, Phi Beta Kappa, and the American Association of Colleges and Schools of Business (AACSB) can be valuable tools for assessing the needs of an institution.

Creating a Sense of Urgency

Because our natural instinct is to resist change, a sense of alarm or urgency oftentimes must be created to effect a needed change. To overcome our innate sense of inertia, the dire consequences of remaining in the status quo need to be articulated by the change agent. There are a number of ways to create a sense of urgency, including citing comparable data from similar institutions and projected student enrollment declines. But in creating a sense of urgency, the change agent must be aware that individuals and groups are often moved by dissimilar forces. In other words, what might cause a sense of urgency in one person might cause a sense of hopelessness in another, which in turn can lead to a self-fulfilling prophesy.

Thus, creating a sense of urgency or stress can have both functional and dysfunctional outcomes. Whether stress takes a constructive or destructive course is influenced by the sociocultural context in which the stress occurs. A culture of trust and respect is a considerable asset.

Effective educational administrators learn how to create functional conflict and manage dysfunctional conflict. They develop and practice techniques for diagnosing the causes and nature of stress and transform it into a productive force that fosters needed change in the institution.

Assessing Favorable and Opposing Forces

Accurate assessment of the forces that affect proposed reform is perhaps the most important step in the integrated change process. Correctly identifying the forces that favor the reform and those that oppose it is crucial to effective implementation of the change. Further, the interventions chosen to neutralize the forces against change and enhance the forces in favor of it are instrumental to its eventual success.

The forces resistant to change can be considerable. These forces range from simple ignorance of an individual to the complex vested interests that exist. As the comic strip character Pogo phrased it, "We have met the enemy and he is us."

The forces resistant to change are an important part of the organization's environment or culture. They must be diagnosed, understood, and taken into account in the targeting process and in selecting a change strategy. According to Richard Carlson, a major organizational feature that contributes to resistance to change is the domestication of public schools and other educational institutions. A domesticated organization has many properties of the monopoly: it does not have to compete for resources, except in a very limited area; it has a steady flow of clients; and its survival is guaranteed. Although private schools and colleges do not possess all of these characteristics in the way that public schools do, many of the teachers view their institutions in this way. One often hears the college professor or the private school teacher proclaim in the light of declining enrollments, "That's the administration's problem" (Carlson 1990).

Force-field Analysis

To understand the changing forces that affect a change, we can use an analytical technique called force-field analysis, which views a problem as a product of forces working in different, often opposite directions. An organization, or any of its subsystems, maintains the status quo when the sum of opposing forces is zero. When forces in one direction exceed forces in the opposite one, the organization or subsystem moves in the direction of the greater forces. For example, if forces for change exceed forces against change, then change is likely to occur (Lewin 1951).

To move the educational institution toward a different desired state requires increasing the forces for change in that direction, decreasing the forces against change in that direction, or both. Generally, reducing resistance forces creates less tension in the system and fewer unanticipated consequences than increasing forces for change. Suppose your institution was moving from homogenous to heterogeneous grouping. Reducing the resistance to the changes created by the introduction of heterogeneous grouping increases the likelihood of the changeover. When the administrators and staff no longer resist change, the present state moves closer to the desired state.

ASSESSMENT OF THE TOLERANCE FOR CHANGE

Consider again our example of heterogeneous grouping. Moving from homogenous grouping in the form of tracking to the more egalitarian heterogeneous grouping is bound to encounter resistance. What are the opposing forces that one can anticipate? Certainly, some of the teaching staff will be against the change because it will entail more small-group instruction and adapting their lesson plans to a variety of ability levels. On the contrary, what are the forces in favor of change? Once again, one can anticipate that certain of the faculty will favor the more inclusive approach that is embodied in heterogeneous grouping. A savvy administrator will be able to apply interventions that would neutralize the opposition and mobilize the forces in favor of this change. Using force-field analysis in a systematic way can be very helpful in bringing about desired change (see figure 10.1). A practical example in the use of the force-field analysis is depicted in table 10.1.

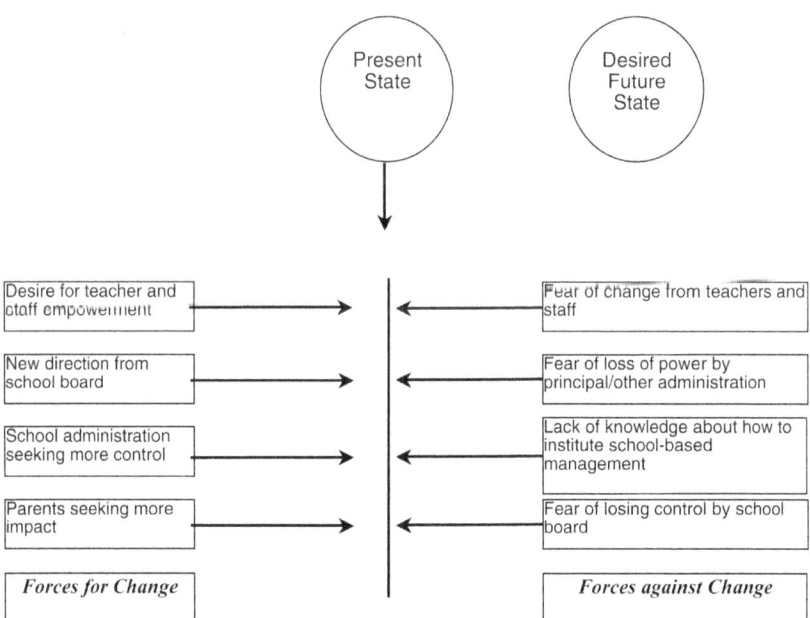

Figure 10.1.   Force-field Analysis Model

Table 10.1. An Example of an Analysis of Target Forces for School-based Management

Target Forces	Alternate Actions
Fear of change by the principal, teachers, and staff	Implement change slowly
	Educate workers about the change
	Illustrate the benefits of the new system
	Pilot-test the system for small groups
	Involve employees in planning the change
Lack of knowledge about how to institute new system	Offer training in culture change
	Provide new policies and procedures

Developing and Selecting Alternatives

While the already-mentioned steps in the integrated change process are being addressed, the change agent should establish a committee or task force of "believers" to begin developing alternatives that would address the perceived need(s). Ideally, a deliberative consideration of the various alternatives should be undertaken, and the ones that best satisfy the cost/benefits analysis should be chosen. All too often, however, "the powers that be" have arbitrarily chosen the preferred alternative and the change agent is expected simply to implement it. This would be an example of what a wise leader never wants to do, namely, "back him- or herself into a corner."

Another phenomenon that sometimes occurs during this phase of the change process is the tendency to "satisfice," or choose the alternative that offends the fewest individuals and/or groups, rather than choose the best alternative. Satisficing is a term coined by Herbert Simon, a Nobel Prize winner in economics, who was critical of the so-called rational model of decision making, which indicates that decision makers develop and analyze all of the possible alternatives and select the best one available (Simon 1960).

According to Simon, at a certain point in the decision-making process, rather than the best-possible alternative being chosen, in the interest of efficiency the decision maker will satisfice, or sacrifice the optimal for a solution or alternative that is satisfactory or good enough. For example, if a school is trying to decide between the traditional phonics approach versus the whole language approach to teaching reading, the change agent(s) may satisfice and choose an integrated model that combines what it believes to be the best aspects of both the phonics and whole language approaches. Thus, the change agent may sacrifice the optimal solution for one that satisfies the greatest number of constituencies.

Promoting a Sense of Ownership

It is a truism in education that if a change or reform is to be implemented successfully, it must have the support and acceptance of the faculty and staff. Consequently, we often hear managers suggest that a new program does not have a chance of succeeding unless the employees take ownership of it. Most of us agree with the common sense of this assertion. But how does a leader effectively promote employee ownership? Let us suggest four steps:

- Respect people. As we have indicated earlier, this starts with appreciating the diverse gifts that individuals bring to your organization. The key is to dwell on the strengths of your coworkers, rather than on their weaknesses.
- Let belief guide policy and practice. We spoke earlier of developing a culture of civility in an institution. If there is an environment of mutual respect and trust, the institution will flourish. Leaders need to let their belief or value systems guide their behavior. Style is merely a consequence of what we believe and what is in our hearts.
- Recognize the need for covenants. Contractual agreements cover such things as salary, fringe benefits, and working conditions. They are part of organization life, and there is a legitimate need for them. But in today's educational institutions, where the best people working in our schools are similar to volunteers, we need covenantal relationships. Our best workers might choose their employers. They usually choose the institution where they work based on reasons less tangible than salaries and fringe benefits. Covenantal relationships enable educational institutions to be civil and hospitable and are understanding of individuals' differences and unique natures.
- Understand that culture counts more than structure. An educational institution recently went through a particularly traumatic time when

the credibility of the administration was questioned by the faculty and staff. Various organizational development consultants were interviewed to facilitate a healing process. Most of the consultants spoke of making the necessary structural changes to create a culture of trust. The consultant who was hired, however, began with the attitude that organizational structure has nothing to do with building trust. Interpersonal relations based on mutual respect and an atmosphere of goodwill are what create a culture of trust.

Providing Staff Development

Very often, staff development, an essential part of the change process, is neglected or overlooked completely. Many educational reforms have failed because of an enthusiastic but ill-advised leader who has tried to implement a change before engaging in staff development. Sometimes, even when staff development is provided, it is poor staff development. Negative responses to staff development are often the result of a history of poor experiences with activities such as in-service training.

The most important resource in an institution is its staff. When the staff's thinking is congruent with organizational needs and when the staff is well-trained, adaptive, and motivated, effective schools result. To achieve this goal requires attention to the various ways in which human potential can be realized and to the variety of needs that any particular person and group might have at any particular stage of development. Providing adequate and effective staff development enables individuals to reach their potential; it enables them to succeed.

Operationalizing Change

At this point in the integrated change process we operationalize the change, or give form to our vision. Although careful preparation for change increases the chances of success, it does not guarantee effective action. Placing the plan in operation requires the establishment of the organizational structure that will best suit the change, and development of an assessment process to determine if the change is remaining on course. Briefing sessions, special seminars, or other means of information dissemination must permeate the change effort. Operationalizing the change must include procedures for keeping all participants informed about the change activities and its effects.

Evaluating Change

The next step in the integrated change process is the evaluation of the change. Authentic assessment is a topical issue in education these days. Many are questioning exactly how to assess performance most accurately, effectively, and fairly. After generations of focusing on program inputs, stressing program *outcomes* as an authentic measure of a program's effectiveness is gaining in popularity. An emphasis on outcomes versus inputs is much preferred in assessing the true effectiveness of a change or reform.

The change agent(s) should collect data about the nature and effectiveness of the change. The results of the evaluation indicate whether the change process is complete, or a return to an earlier stage should occur. The criteria for success should be specified in advance of a change effort. These criteria can be culturally linked and varied; they also should be closely related to the *goals* of the reform. If ineffective outcomes result from the introduction of a whole language-based reading program, for example, the process should return to an earlier stage, such as needs assessment, to determine if the institution is really in need of it, and if the school community has been properly prepared.

Institutionalizing Change

Provided that the evaluation process shows that the reform has been effective, the change then should become institutionalized that is, the changed processes and/or programs should be established as permanent ways of operating. Otherwise, when the current change agent(s) leaves, the change may not be perpetuated. Ideally, the reform should become part of the organizational culture. It is in this way that a legacy is created from which future generations of students, parents, faculty, and staff can benefit. The results of a failure to institutionalize a reform are often seen at the state and federal department of education levels. How many times have we seen a governor or president set an effective educational agenda, only to have it scuttled and replaced with a different agenda by the subsequent administration? If a successful change is to prevail over time, it must be institutionalized.

CHAPTER 10

Educational leaders, therefore, must build learning communities, ones that emphasize ongoing adaptability and self-generation, thereby emphasizing coping and looking at the world creatively. Peter Senge says, "Leaders in learning organizations are responsible for building organizations where people are continually expanding their capabilities to shape their future—that is, leaders are responsible for learning" (Senge 1990). Where better to implement Senge's ideas regarding a learning community than in an educational institution?

Conclusion

W. Edwards Deming said that healthy organizations are ones that are continually improving. Continuous improvement assumes change. Therefore, if an educational leader is to be effective, he or she must become an agent of change (Deming 2000).

Mastering the change process requires a leader to know and understand the steps involved in planning a successful transformation in an organization. If the change can take place in an atmosphere of mutual trust and respect, its chances for success are maximized.

The suggested model for effecting change is to access the organization to ascertain the need for change, to diagnose the forces that influence change, and to implement the change by maximizing the forces in favor of the change and minimizing the forces opposing the change.

Once the change is made, a thorough evaluation of its effectiveness precedes the final step of institutionalizing the change, which ensures its continuation—even after the change agent is no longer present.

A key step in the process is the diagnosing of the forces influencing change. A useful technique in assessing these factors is called force-field analysis. This technique allows one to determine the forces in favor and opposed to change and to plan interventions that would mobilize the forces in favor of change and mitigate the forces opposing change. If one can effectively orchestrate this step of the process, the desired change will most likely occur. In many ways, successfully effecting a transformational change necessitates the collective use of all of an administrator's knowledge and skills. It can be seen as the culminating activity of an educational leader.

Diagnostic Checklist

Here are some questions that can be addressed in assessing an institution's ability to change:

- Are all the steps of the integrated change model being implemented?
- Is a force-field analysis used during the change process?
- Are the intervention strategies appropriate for the situation?
- Do mechanisms exist for institutionalizing the change?

ONE-MINUTE ASSESSMENT OF LEADING WITH HEART

Do unto others what you would have them do unto you.

—*The Golden Rule*

How the leader utilizes the concepts contained in the preceding chapters of this book depends largely on his or her philosophy regarding how human beings behave in the workplace. The two extremes of the continuum might be described as those leaders who believe that human beings are basically lazy and will do the very least that they need to do to "get by" in the workplace. Or those who believe that people are basically industrious and, if given the choice, would opt for doing a quality job. I believe that today's most effective leaders hold the latter view. I agree with Max De Pree, former owner and CEO of the highly successful Herman Miller Furniture Company. Writing in his book *Leadership Is an Art*, he says that a leader's function is to "liberate people to do what is required of them in the most effective and humane way possible" (De Pree 1989). Instead of catching people doing something wrong, our goal as enlightened leaders is to catch them doing something right. I would suggest, therefore, that in addition to a rational approach to leadership (leading with *mind*), a truly enlightened leader leads with heart.

CHAPTER 11

Too often, leaders underestimate the skills and qualities of their followers. I remember Bill Faries, the chief custodian at a high school at which I was assistant principal in the mid-1970s. Bill's mother, with whom he had been extraordinarily close, had passed away after a long illness. The school was religiously affiliated and the school community went "all out" in its remembrance of Bill's mother. We held a religious service in which almost 3,000 members of the school community participated. Bill, of course, was very grateful. As a token of his gratitude he gave the school a 6-by-8-foot quilt that he had personally knitted. From that point on, I did not know if Bill was a custodian who was a quilt weaver, or a quilt weaver who was a custodian. The point is that it took the death of his mother for me and others to realize how truly talented our custodian was. So, our effectiveness as leaders begins with an understanding of the diversity of people's gifts, talents, and skills. When we think about the variety of gifts that people bring to organizations and institutions, we see that leading with heart lies in cultivating, liberating, and enabling those gifts.

LEADERSHIP DEFINED

The first responsibility of a leader is to define reality through a vision. The last is to say thank you. In between, the leader must become the servant of the servants. Being a leader means having the opportunity to make a meaningful difference in the lives of those who allow leaders to lead. In a nutshell, leaders who lead with heart don't inflict pain; they bear pain.

Whether one is a successful leader can be determined by looking at the followers. Are they reaching their potential? Are they learning? Are they able to change without bitterness? Are they able to achieve the institution's goals and objectives? Can they manage conflict among themselves? Where the answers to these questions are an emphatic "yes" is where a leader with heart resides.

I prefer to think about leadership in terms of what the gospel writer Luke calls the "one who serves." The leader owes something to the institution he or she leads. The leader is seen in this context as steward rather than owner or proprietor. Leading with heart requires the leader to think about his or her stewardship in terms of legacy, values, direction, and effectiveness.

Legacy

Too many of today's leaders are interested only in immediate results that bolster their career goals. Long-range goals are left to their successors. I believe that this approach fosters autocratic leadership, which oftentimes produces short-term results but militates against creativity and its long-term benefits. In effect, this approach is the antithesis of leading with heart.

On the contrary, leaders should build a long-lasting legacy of accomplishment that is institutionalized for posterity. They owe their institutions and their followers a healthy existence and the relationships and reputation that enable continuity of that healthy existence. Leaders are also responsible for future leadership succession. They need to identify, develop, and nurture future leaders to carry on the legacy.

Values

Along with being responsible for providing future leaders, leaders owe the individuals in their institutions certain other legacies. Leaders need to be concerned with the institutional value system that determines the principles and standards that guide the practices of those in the organization. Leaders need to model their value systems so that the individuals in the organization can learn to transmit these values to their colleagues and to future employees. In a civilized institution, we see good manners, respect for people, and an appreciation of the way in which we serve one another. A humane, sensitive, and thoughtful leader will transmit his or her value system through his or her daily behavior.

Direction

Leaders are obliged to provide and maintain direction by developing a vision. We made the point earlier that effective leaders must leave their organizations with a legacy. Part of this legacy should be a sense of progress or momentum. An educational administrator, for instance, should imbue his or her institution with a sense of continuous progress, a sense of constant improvement. Improvement and momentum come from a clear vision of what the institution ought to be, from a well-planned strategy to achieve that vision, and from carefully developed and articulated directions and plans that allow everyone to participate and feel personally accountable for achieving those plans.

Effectiveness

Leaders are also responsible for effectiveness by being enablers. They need to enable others to reach their potential both personally and institutionally. I believe that the most effective ways of enabling one's colleagues is through participative decision making. It begins with believing in the potential of people, believing in their diversity of gifts. Leaders must realize that to maximize their own power and effectiveness, they need to empower others. Leaders are responsible for setting and attaining the goals in their organizations. Empowering or enabling others to help achieve those goals enhances the leader's chances of attaining those goals, ultimately enhancing the leader's effectiveness and power. Paradoxically, giving up power really amounts to gaining power.

IT STARTS WITH TRUST AND RESPECT

These are exciting times in education. Revolutionary steps are being taken to restructure schools and rethink the teaching-learning process. The concepts of empowerment, total quality management, the use of technology, and strategic planning are becoming the norm. However, although these activities have the potential to influence education in significantly positive ways, they must be based upon a strong foundation to achieve their full potential.

Achieving educational effectiveness is an incremental, sequential improvement process. This improvement process begins by building a sense of security within each individual so that he or she can be flexible in adapting to changes within education. Addressing only skills or techniques, such as communication, motivation, negotiation, or empowerment, is ineffective when individuals in an organization do not trust its systems, themselves, or each other. An institution's resources are wasted when invested only in training programs that assist teacher and staff in mastering quick-fix techniques that at best attempt to manipulate and at worst reinforce mistrust.

The challenge is to transform relationships based on insecurity, adversity, and politics to those based on mutual trust. Trust is the beginning of effectiveness and forms the foundation of a principle-centered learning environment that places emphasis upon strengths and devises innovative methods to minimize weaknesses. The transformation process requires an internal locus of control that emphasizes individual responsibility and accountability for change and for promoting effectiveness.

TEAMWORK

For many of us, there exists a dichotomy between how we see ourselves as persons and how we see ourselves as workers. We began chapter 1 of this book with the words of a Zen Buddhist:

> The master in the art of living makes little distinction
> between his work and his play, his labor and his leisure,
> his mind and his body, his education and his recreation,
> his love and his religion. He hardly knows which is which.
> He simply pursues his vision of excellence in whatever he does,
> leaving others to decide whether he is working or playing.
> To him he is always doing both.

Work can be and should be productive, rewarding, enriching, fulfilling, and joyful. Work is one of our greatest privileges, and it is up to leaders to make certain that work is everything that it can and should be.

Paramount among the ideals that leaders need to recognize in leading an organization is the notion of teamwork and the valuing of each individual's contribution to the final product. The synergy produced by an effective team is greater than the sum of its parts.

The foundation of the team is the recognition that each member needs every other member and no individual can be successful without the cooperation of others. As a young boy, I was a very enthusiastic baseball fan. My favorite player was the Hall of Fame pitcher Robin Roberts of the Philadelphia Phillies. During the early 1950s, his fastball dominated the National League. My uncle, who took me to my first ballgame, explained that opposing batters were so intimidated by Roberts's fastball that they were automatic "outs" even before they got to the plate. My uncle claimed that Robin Roberts was unstoppable. Even as a young boy, I intuitively knew

CHAPTER 11

that no one was unstoppable by himself. I said to my uncle that I knew how to stop Robin Roberts. "Make me his catcher!"

EMPLOYEES AS VOLUNTEERS

Our institutions will not amount to anything without the people who make them what they are. And the individuals most influential in making institutions what they are are essentially volunteers. Our very best employees can work anywhere they please. So, in a sense, they volunteer to work where they do. As leaders, we would do far better if we looked upon and treated our employees as volunteers. We made the point earlier that we should treat our employees as if we had a covenantal relationship rather than a contractual relationship with them.

Alexander Solzhenitsyn, speaking to the 1978 graduating class of Harvard College, said this about legalistic relationships: "a society based on the letter of the law and never reaching any higher, fails to take advantage of the full range of human possibilities. The letter of the law is too cold and formal to have a beneficial influence on society. Whenever the tissue of life is woven of legalistic relationships, this creates an atmosphere of spiritual mediocrity that paralyzes men's noblest impulses." And later: "After a certain level of the problem has been reached, legalistic thinking induces paralysis; it prevents one from seeing the scale and the meaning of events" (Solzhenitsyn 1978).

Covenantal relationships, on the other hand, induce freedom, not paralysis. As the noted psychiatrist William Glasser explains, "coercion only produces mediocrity; love or a sense of belonging produces excellence" (Glasser 1984). Our goal as leaders is to encourage a covenantal relationship of love, warmth, and personal chemistry among our employee volunteers. Shared ideals, shared goals, shared respect, a sense of integrity, a sense of quality, a sense of advocacy, and a sense of caring—these are the basis of an organization's covenant with its employees.

EMPLOYEE OWNERS

If an educational institution is to be successful, everyone in it needs to feel that he or she "owns the place." "This is not the school district's school; it is not the school board's school; it is my school." Taking ownership is a sign of one's love for an institution. In his book *The Servant as Leader*, Robert Greenleaf says, "Love is an indefinable term, and its manifestations are both subtle and infinite. It has only one absolute condition: unlimited liability!" Although it might run counter to our traditional notion of American capitalism, employees should be encouraged to act as if they own the place. It is a sign of love (Greenleaf 2008).

THE IGNATIAN VISION

An alternative lens through which we can view our leadership behavior to be certain that we are leading with heart is the Ignation vision. More than 450 years ago Ignatius of Loyola, a young priest born to a Spanish aristocratic family, founded the Society of Jesus, the Jesuits, and wrote his seminal book, *The Spiritual Exercises* (Loyola 2007).

In this book, he suggested a "way of life" and a "way of looking at things" that has been propagated by his religious community and his other followers for almost five centuries. His principles have been utilized in a variety of ways. They have been used as an aid in developing one's own spiritual life; they have been used to formulate a way of learning that has become the curriculum and instructional method employed in the more than sixty high schools and the twenty-eight Jesuit colleges and universities in the United States; and they have been used to develop one's own administrative style. Together, these principles comprise the Ignatian vision.

There are five Ignatian principles that we will explore here as a foundation for developing a moral frame that could guide our leadership behavior to ensure that we are leading with heart: (1) Ignatius's concept of the *magis*, or the "more." (2) The implications of his notion of *cura personalis*, or "care of the person." (3) The process of *discernment*. (4) The development of *men and women for others*. (5) And his concept of *social justice*.

At the core of the Ignatian vision is the concept of the *magis*, or the "more." Ignatius spent the greater part of his life seeking perfection in all areas of his personal, spiritual, and professional life. He was never satisfied with the status quo. He was constantly seeking to improve his own spiritual life, as well as his secular life as leader of a growing religious community. He was an advocate of "continuous improvement" long before it became a corporate slogan, and long before people like Edwards Deming used it to develop his total quality management approach to management, and long before Japan used it to revolutionize its economy after World War II.

The idea of constantly seeking "the more" implies change. The *magis* is a movement away from the status quo, and moving away from the status quo defines change. The Ignatian vision requires individuals and institutions to embrace the process of change as a vehicle for personal and institutional improvement. For his followers, frontiers and boundaries are not obstacles or ends, but new challenges to be faced, new opportunities to be welcomed.

Thus, change needs to become a way of life. Ignatius further implores his followers to "be the change that you expect in others." In other words, we are called to model desired behavior—to live out our values, to be of ever fuller service to our communities and to aspire to the more universal good. Ignatius had no patience with mediocrity. He constantly strove for the greater good.

Closely related to the principle of the *magis* is the Ignatian principle of discernment. In his writings, he urges us to challenge the status quo through the process of discernment. To Ignatius, the need to enter into the discernment process is to better determine God's will. However, this process is of value for the purely *secular* purpose of deciding on which "horn of a dilemma" one should come down—the preferred horn would be the one that best serves the common good.

Ignatius presents us with several other supplemental norms for facing our "dilemmas." In choices that directly affect the individual person and the underserved or marginalized, especially the poor, Ignatius urges us to give preference to those in need. This brings us to his next guiding principle, *cura personalis*, or care of the person.

Another of Ignatius's important and enduring principles is his notion that, despite the primacy of the common good, the need to care for the individual person should never be lost. From the very beginning, the *cura personalis* principle has been included in the mission statement of virtually every high school and college founded by the Jesuits. It also impacts the method of instruction suggested for all Jesuit schools in the *Ratio Studiorum*, or the "course of study" in these institutions. Thus, a Jesuit education is primarily student centered rather than teacher centered.

All Jesuit educational institutions are to foster what we now refer to as a "constructivist" classroom, where the student is an active participant in the learning process. This contrasts with the "transmission" method of instruction where the teacher is paramount, and the student is a passive participant in the process.

This principle also has implications for how we conduct ourselves as educational administrators. Ignatius calls us to value the gifts and charisms of our colleagues and to address any deficiencies that they might have and turn them into strengths. For example, during the employee evaluation process, Ignatius would urge us to focus on the formative or developmental stage of the evaluation far more than on the summative or employment decision stage. This would be one small way of placing *cura personalis* theory into practice.

The fourth principle that we wish to consider is the Ignatian concept of service. Once again, this principle has been propagated from the very outset. The expressed goal of virtually every Jesuit institution is "to develop men and women with and for others." Jesuit institutions are called on to create a culture of service as one way of ensuring that the students, faculty, and staffs of these institutions reflect the educational, civic, and spiritual values of the Ignatian vision.

The implications of "service to others" for administration are clear. Educational administrators enhance their effectiveness not only by including the idea of service to others in their curricula, but also by modeling it in their personal and professional lives. Assuming the role of the "servant of the servants" is what we are suggesting. Servant leaders do not inflict pain, they bear pain, and they treat their employees as "volunteers," a concept explored earlier.

The Ignatian concept of "service" transitions rather easily into his notion of solidarity with the underserved and marginalized, or his principle of *social justice*. According to some, Ignatius defined justice in both a narrow and wide sense (Toner 1991). In the narrow sense, it is "justice among men and women" that is involved. In this case, it is a matter of "clear obligations" among "members of the human family." The application of this kind of justice would include not only the rendering of material goods, but also immaterial goods such as "reputation, dignity, the possibility of exercising freedom" (Tripole 1994).

Many of his followers also believe Ignatius defined justice in a wider sense "where situations are encountered which are humanly intolerable and demand a remedy" (Tripole 1994). Here the situations may be a product of "explicitly unjust acts" caused by "clearly identified people" who cannot be commanded to correct the injustices, yet the dignity of the human person requires that justice be restored; or they may be caused by non-identifiable people.

It is precisely within the structural forces of inequality in society where injustice of this second type is found, where injustice is "institutionalized," that is, built into economic, social, and political structures both national and international, and where people are suffering from poverty and hunger, from the unjust distribution of wealth, resources, and power.

It is almost certain that Ignatius did not only concern himself with injustices that were purely economic. He often cites injustices about "threats to human life and its quality," "racial and political discrimination," and loss of respect for the "rights of individuals or groups" (Chapple 1993). When one adds to these the "vast range of injustices" enumerated in his writings, one sees that the Ignatian vision understands its mission of justice to include "the widest possible view of justice," involving every area where there is an attack on human rights. The concepts of leading with mind and heart through the Ignatian vision are depicted in figure 11.1, which I call the "Cura Wheel."

IMPLICATIONS FOR ADMINISTRATION

Each of the principles of the Ignatian vision noted above has a variety of implications for leaders. The *magis* principle calls on us to continually seek perfection in all that we do. In effect, this means that we must seek to continually improve, always striving for the greater good. And, since improvement implies change, we need to be agents of needed change in our institutions. This means that we have to model a tolerance for change and embrace not only our own change initiatives, but also those in other parts of the institution. In effect, the Ignatian vision prompts not only leaders but transformational leaders.

The principle of *cura personalis* has additional implications. To practice the Ignatian vision, one must treat people with human dignity and civility under all circumstances. Being sensitive to individuals' unique needs is

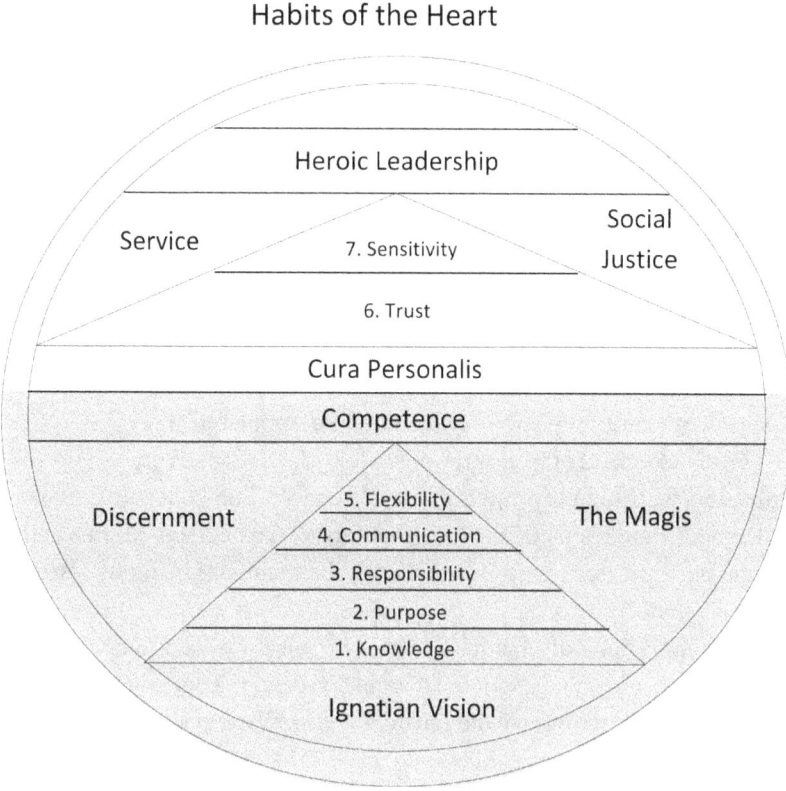

Figure 11.1. Cura Wheel

particularly required. At times in our efforts to treat people equally, we fail to treat them fairly or equitably. Some individuals have greater needs than others, and many times these needs require exceptions to be made on their behalf.

For example, if a colleague does not complete an assignment on time, but the tardiness is due to the fact that he or she is going through some personal or family trauma at the moment, the principle of *cura personalis* calls on us to make an exception in this case. It is likely that some would consider such an exception to be unfair to those who made the effort to complete their assignments in a timely manner or object to it because "we cannot be all things to all people." However, as long as the exception is made for everyone in the same circumstances, Ignatius would not believe the exception to be unfair.

The Ignatian process of *discernment* requires educational administrators to be reflective practitioners. It calls on us to be introspective regarding our administrative and leadership behavior. We are asked to reflect on the ramifications of our decisions, especially in light of their cumulative effect on the equitable distribution of power and on the marginalized individuals and groups in our institutions. In effect, the principle of discernment galvanizes the other principles embodied in the Ignatian vision. During the discernment process, we are asked to reflect upon how our planned behavior will manifest the *magis* principle, *cura personalis*, and service to the community, especially the underserved, marginalized, and oppressed.

The development of men and women for others requires one to approach leadership with humility and a spirit of service. The concept of "servant leadership" requires us to encourage others toward a life of service and to assume our own leadership position with the mantle of being the "servant of the servants."

The implications of Ignatius's notion of social justice are myriad for a leader. Being concerned about the marginalized among our constituencies is a requirement of followers of the Ignatian vision. We are called to be particularly sensitive to those individuals and groups that do not share equitably in the distribution of power and influence. In a school setting, these persons might be the secretaries and the custodians, or even the parents. Distinctions according to race, class, gender, and status should be corrected. Participative decision making and collaborative behavior are expected among administrators imbued with the Ignatian vision. Thus, in my view, a moral frame like the Ignatian vision *completes* situational leadership theory by enabling leaders to lead with heart. Left on its own, situational leadership theory is secular and amoral. Utilizing situational leadership theory alone, that is, leading only with one's mind, is as likely to produce a leader in the mold of Adolph Hitler as it is to produce a leader in the mold of Abraham Lincoln. But by using the additional lens of the Ignatian vision or some other moral code through which to view our leadership behavior, I believe that our society will experience more leaders like Lincoln and fewer like Hitler.

ONE-MINUTE ASSESSMENT OF LEADING WITH HEART

DIAGNOSTIC CHECKLIST

If the following conditions are prevalent in your institution, the leaders are most likely not *leading with heart*:

- There is a tendency to merely "go through the motions."
- A dark tension exists among key individuals or groups.
- A cynical attitude prevails.
- Finding time to celebrate accomplishments becomes problematic.
- There is the view that one person's gain needs to be at another's expense.
- Leaders accumulate power rather than share it.
- Attainment of short-term goals is preferred to the acquisition of long-term goals.
- Individuals abide by the letter of the law, but not the spirit.
- Educators treat students as impositions.
- The accidents become more important than the essence.
- The loss of grace, style, and civility occur.
- Leaders use coercion to motivate employees.
- Administrators dwell on individuals' weaknesses rather than their strengths.
- Individual turf is protected to the detriment of institutional goals.
- Diversity and individual charisms are not respected.
- Communication is only one way.
- Employees feel exploited and manipulated.
- Arrogance spawns top-down decision making.
- Leaders prefer to be served rather than to serve.

WHAT HAVE WE LEARNED?

The greatest discovery of my generation is that man can alter his life simply by altering his attitude of mind.

—William James

INTRODUCTION

What have we learned about organizational development and leadership in the last eleven chapters of this book? First, we learned a systematic way of diagnosing an institution's organizational health, namely by constantly assessing the eleven components of an organization. Second, we gained the knowledge and skills to address any weaknesses that we found. We also found that situational or contingency leadership theory makes common sense. Today's leaders and aspiring leaders need to be able to adapt their leadership behavior to changing situations. None of us can afford to be "stuck" in one paradigm. The truly heroic leaders among us are successful because they are able to very effectively balance their use of the four leadership frames enunciated by Lee Bolman and Terrence Deal, while filtering all of one's leadership behavior through a moral frame. Finally, we learned the importance of organizational development and leadership theory.

CHAPTER 12

THE IMPORTANCE OF THEORY

We cannot underestimate the value and importance of theory in the field of organizational development and leadership, or in any other field for that matter. Without theory we have no valid way of diagnosing, analyzing, and correcting failed practice. Without a theoretical base, we oftentimes lead by trial and error, or by the proverbial "seat of our pants."

Theory is to leadership as fundamentals are to athletics. For example, if a basketball player is suddenly shooting a lower percentage than his or her career average, something is obviously wrong. He or she has experienced "failed practice." What to do? Most athletes in this situation are coached to "go back to the basics" or the fundamentals. The basketball player will review the fundamentals of shooting, like squaring oneself to the basket, keeping the shooting elbow in, keeping the guide-hand off the ball upon release, snapping the wrist, and exaggerating one's follow-through. It is likely that one or more of these fundamentals is being violated and causing the shooting percentage decline and, when corrected, the percentage will rise again to its most recent average.

If the athlete does not know the fundamentals of shooting, or *shooting theory* if you will, he or she can only correct the problem through the very inefficient means of trial and error. The same goes for leaders who are losing their impact on their followers. If they have not adopted a leadership theory to guide their behavior, they can only correct the leadership decline by trial and error.

However, if the leader has internalized a leadership theory, the leader can review the tenets or principles of the theory and most likely diagnose the deficiency and correct it rather quickly. For example, the leader might find that his or her followers are no longer responding to the leader's friendly persuasion and active support (human resource leadership behavior). In analyzing the *situation*, the leader might conclude that he or she is using human resource behavior with the followers when structural leadership behavior may be more appropriate. As a result of this analysis, the leader may decide to utilize a more structural approach and "lay down the law" to his recalcitrant followers. This rather simple example demonstrates the importance and value of theory in providing leaders with the knowledge and skills they need to be able to diagnose and correct failed practice in an efficient and effective way.

LEADING WITH MIND

Knowledge of one's field is a sine qua non for effective leadership. This quality usually manifests itself in one's structural frame leadership behavior. In sports terms, the leader must have a good command of the fundamentals of the game. In business terms, the effective leader must have a thorough knowledge of the technical aspects of how a business operates and a sense of how to develop a viable business plan. In education, the leader needs to know how schools and school systems operate and what the best practices in the field are in curriculum and instruction. In a family situation, the leader (parent or guardian) needs to have at least a modicum of knowledge regarding the principles of child psychology. In short, leaders in any field need to know that field and be able to apply that knowledge through the theory and practice of organizational development, which would include the following:

a. Organizational structure: how an institution is organized.
b. Organizational culture: the values and beliefs of an institution.
c. Motivation: the system of rewards and incentives provided.
d. Communication: the clarity and accuracy of the communication process.
e. Decision making: how and by whom decisions are made.
f. Conflict management: how dysfunctional conflict is handled.
g. Power distribution: how the power in an institution is distributed.
h. Strategic planning: how the mission, vision, and strategic plan are developed.
i. Change: how change is effectively implemented in an institution.
j. Leading with heart: whether a culture of trust and respect prevails in an institution.

Included in the appendix is a pair of diagnostic tools entitled "The Heart Smart Survey I and II," which I developed to help leaders assess the organizational health of their institutions. Heart Smart I assesses whether the leaders are leading with *mind* and Heart Smart II assesses whether the leaders are leading with *heart*. Together they identify which of the factors listed above are in need of improvement.

CHAPTER 12

LEADING WITH HEART

To recap, then, the effective leader needs to be *technically* competent. However, being technically competent is not enough. To be truly effective and heroic, leaders need to master the *art* of leadership and learn to lead with *heart*. In effect, leaders need to operate out of both the structural and political frames (science) and the human resources, symbolic, and moral frames (art) to maximize their effectiveness. This means that they must be concerned about the person (*cura personalis*). They must abide by the Golden Rule and treat others as they wish to be treated. As noted earlier, truly effective leaders treat their employees like volunteers and empower them to actualize their true potential, thus engendering mutual trust and respect among their colleagues.

In their book entitled *Leading with Kindness* (2008), William Baker and Michael O'Malley reiterate my views. They explore how one of the most unheralded features of leadership, basic human kindness, drives successful organizations. And while most scholars generally recognize that a leader's emotional intelligence factors into that person's leadership behavior, most are reticent to consider it to be as important as analytical ability, decision-making skills, or implementation skills. Such emotions as compassion, empathy, and kindness are often dismissed as unquantifiable and are often seen as weaknesses. Yet research in neuroscience and the social sciences clearly reveals that one's physiological and emotional states have measurable effects on both individual and group performance.

In the jargon of the day, individuals who lead with heart or kindness are said to have a high degree of emotional intelligence. Most of us are familiar with the current notion of multiple intelligences; that is, individuals have a number of intelligences in addition to cognitive intelligence. Among these intelligences is emotional intelligence. Several theories within the emotional intelligence paradigm seek to understand how individuals perceive, understand, utilize, and manage emotions in an effort to predict and foster personal effectiveness.

Most of these models define emotional intelligence as an array of traits and abilities related to emotional and social knowledge that influence our overall ability to effectively cope with environmental demands; as such, it can be viewed as a model of psychological well-being and adaptation. This includes the ability to be aware of, to understand, and to relate to others; the ability to deal with strong emotions and to control one's impulses; and the ability to adapt to change and to solve problems of a personal and social nature. The five main domains of these models are intrapersonal skills, interpersonal skills, adaptability, stress management, and general mood. If the reader sees a similarity between emotional intelligence and what I term *leading with heart* and what Baker and O'Malley call *leading with kindness*, it is not coincidental.

LEADING WITH MIND AND HEART

So, the truly heroic leaders lead with *both* mind (science) and heart (art)—with cognitive intelligence and emotional intelligence. One or the other will not suffice. Only by mastering both will the leader succeed. For example, former president William Clinton was rendered ineffective as a leader because of the Monica Lewinsky affair and was nearly impeached. Why? Because he suddenly lost the *knowledge* of how government works (science)? No! He lost his ability to lead because he lost the *trust and respect* of much of the American public (art). He could still lead with his mind, but he had lost the ability to lead with heart. It is only recently, more than a decade later, that he is reestablishing his integrity with the American public.

On the contrary, one could argue that former president Jimmy Carter lost his ability to lead because of a perceived lack of competency. Rightly or wrongly, the majority of the voting public did not believe that he had the knowledge necessary to manage government operations and effectively lead with mind. However, virtually no one questioned his concern for people, his integrity, and his ability to lead with heart. Absent the perceived ability to do *both*, however, he lost the 1980 election to Ronald Reagan.

I conclude, then, that effective leaders are situational; that is, they are capable of adapting their leadership behavior to the situation. They utilize structural, human resources, symbolic, political, and moral leadership behavior when appropriate. They lead with both mind (structural and political behavior) and with heart (human resources, symbolic, and moral behavior). They master both the science (mind) and art (heart) of leadership, and in doing so, they are transformational, leading their organizations to new

CHAPTER 12

heights. As Chris Lowney (2003) writes in *Heroic Leadership*, such leaders are, in a word, truly "heroic."

CONCLUSION

What I have attempted to do in this book is to provide a corollary to Blanchard and Johnson's *One Minute Manager* by suggesting that taking ten minutes each day to assess eleven important components or aspects of one's institution is a worthwhile and productive exercise. Together, these components complete the jigsaw puzzle of effective school management and if mastered will go a long way toward making our institutions places to which we and our colleagues look forward to coming day after day—places where teachers teach well and learners learn well.

APPENDIX: DIAGNOSTICS

THE HEART SMART SURVEY I AND II

Just as there are vital signs in measuring individual health, it is believed that there are vital signs for measuring the health of educational institutions. This survey (Heart Smart Survey I) will help to identify those vital signs in your school or school system. It, along with The Heart Smart Survey II, will indicate further whether the institution's leaders are leading with both mind and heart.

The Heart Smart Survey I

Please think of your *present work environment* and indicate the degree to which you agree or disagree with each of the following statements. A "1" is *Agree Strongly* and a "7" is *Disagree Strongly*.

Disagree Strongly	Disagree	Disagree Slightly	Neither Agree nor Disagree	Agree Slightly	Agree	Agree Strongly
7	6	5	4	3	2	1

APPENDIX: DIAGNOSTICS

1. The manner in which the tasks in this institution are divided is a logical one.
2. The relationships among co-workers are harmonious.
3. This institution's leadership efforts result in its fulfillment of its purposes.
4. My work at this institution offers me an opportunity to grow as a person.
5. I can always talk to someone at work, if I have a work-related problem.
6. The faculty actively participates in decisions.
7. There is little evidence of unresolved conflict in this institution.
8. There is a strong fit between this institution's mission and my own values.
9. The faculty and staff are represented on most committees and task forces.
10. Staff development routinely accompanies any significant changes that occur in this institution.
11. The manner in which the tasks in this institution are distributed is a fair one.
12. Older faculty's opinions are valued.
13. The administrators display the behaviors required for effective leadership.
14. The rewards and incentives here are both internal and external.
15. There is open and direct communication among all levels of this institution.
16. Participative decision making is fostered at this institution.
17. What little conflict that exists at this institution is not dysfunctional.
18. Representatives of all segments of the school community participate in the strategic planning process.
19. The faculty and staff have an appropriate voice in the operation of this institution.
20. This institution is not resistant to constructive change.
21. The division of labor in this organization helps its efforts to reach its goals.
22. I feel valued by this institution.

APPENDIX: DIAGNOSTICS

23. The administration encourages an appropriate amount of participation in decision making.
24. Faculty and staff members are often recognized for special achievements.
25. There are no significant barriers to effective communication at this institution.
26. When the *acceptance* of a decision is important, a group decision-making model is used.
27. There are mechanisms at this institution to effectively manage conflict and stress.
28. Most of the employees understand the mission and goals of this institution.
29. The faculty and staff feel empowered to make their own decisions regarding their daily work.
30. Tolerance toward change is modeled by the administration of this institution.
31. The various grade level teachers and departments work well together.
32. Differences among people are accepted.
33. The leadership is able to generate continuous improvement in the institution.
34. My ideas are encouraged, recognized, and used.
35. Communication is carried out in a non-aggressive style.
36. In general, the decision-making process is an effective one.
37. Conflicts are usually resolved before they become dysfunctional.
38. For the most part, the employees of this institution feel an "ownership" of its goals.
39. The faculty and staff are encouraged to be creative in their work.
40. When changes are made they do so within a rational process.
41. This institution's organizational design responds well to changes in the internal and external environment
42. The teaching and the non-teaching staffs get along with one another.
43. The leadership of this institution espouses a clear educational vision.
44. The goals and objectives for the year are mutually developed by the faculty and the administration.

APPENDIX: DIAGNOSTICS

45. I believe that my opinions and ideas are listened to.
46. Usually, a collaborative style of decision making is utilized at this institution.
47. A collaborative approach to conflict resolution is ordinarily used.
48. This institution has a clear educational vision.
49. The faculty and staff can express their opinions without fear of retribution.
50. I feel confident that I will have an opportunity for input if a significant change were to take place in this institution.
51. This institution is "people-oriented."
52. Administrators and faculty have mutual respect for one another.
53. Administrators give people the freedom to do their job.
54. The rewards and incentives in this institution are designed to satisfy a variety of individual needs.
55. The opportunity for feedback is always available in the communications process.
56. Group decision-making techniques, like brainstorming and group surveys are sometimes used in the decision-making process.
57. Conflicts are oftentimes prevented by early intervention.
58. This institution has a strategic plan for the future.
59. Most administrators here use the power of persuasion rather than the power of coercion.
60. This institution is committed to continually improving through the process of change.
61. This institution does not adhere to a strict chain of command.
62. This institution exhibits grace, style, and civility.
63. The administrators model desired behavior.
64. At this institution, employees are not normally coerced into doing things.
65. I have the information that I need to do a good job.
66. I can constructively challenge the decisions in this institution.
67. A process to resolve work-related grievances is available.
68. There is an ongoing planning process at this institution.
69. The faculty and staff have input into the operation of this institution through a collective bargaining unit or through a faculty governance body.

APPENDIX: DIAGNOSTICS

70. The policies, procedures, and programs of this institution are periodically reviewed.

The Heart Smart Survey II

Please think of your *present work environment* and indicate the degree to which you agree or disagree with each of the following statements. A "1" is *Agree Strongly* and a "7" is *Disagree Strongly*.

Disagree Strongly	Disagree	Disagree Slightly	Neither Agree nor Disagree	Agree Slightly	Agree	Agree Strongly
7	6	5	4	3	2	1

1. There is not much evidence of faculty and staff holding and espousing ethical values.
2. There is not much evidence of mutual respect and understanding among the faculty and staff.
3. There is not much of a sense of voluntarism and dedication among the teachers and staff.
4. There is not much indication that teachers and staff have committed themselves to the modeling of moral and ethical values.
5. There is not much trust and respect shared among faculty, staff, and administration.
6. There is little evidence that teachers encourage students to be concerned for the underserved in their communities.
7. There is not much evidence that the teachers are supportive of a moral or ethical code to guide one's behavior.
8. There are not many occasions when the faculty and staff get to interact with one another.
9. There are not many opportunities presented to students to develop an appreciation of and respect for cultures other than their own.
10. Teachers do not often bear witness to their values and beliefs through their daily behavior.
11. The faculty and staff do not seem to support one another in various events and activities.

APPENDIX: DIAGNOSTICS

12. There are not many occasions when faculty members accompany their students on community service activities.
13. There are no occasions when faculty and students discuss their values and beliefs.
14. There is not much in the way of promotion of justice and fairness among students.
15. There is not a culture that fosters service to the community at this institution.
16. The faculty does not seem to go out of its way to model their belief system to the students.
17. There is not much evidence of the promotion of justice and fairness among teachers.
18. There are not many occasions when teachers engage in community service by donating space, time, resources, and personal help.
19. There are not many times when the faculty and staff articulate or speak out on their values and beliefs.
20. There is not much evidence of the promotion of justice and fairness between teachers and administrators.
21. There are not many instances of faculty evidencing compassion and giving service to the needy, the disadvantaged, and troubled students and co-workers.
22. There are not many occasions when the faculty discusses teaching values and ethics.
23. There are significant barriers to effective communication at this institution.
24. The overall morale of the school is not very good.
25. The faculty and staff do not show much concern for world problems, like hunger, poverty, war, pollution, and social justice.
26. The faculty does not openly express its support of ethical and moral values.
27. The conflicts that arise among individuals and groups are not resolved very well.
28. The teachers do not encourage a sense of service and social justice in their students very much.
29. The faculty do not avail themselves of professional development opportunities to develop their skills in teaching values education.

APPENDIX: DIAGNOSTICS

30. The sense of trust and respect at this institution is not very high.
31. There is a tendency to merely "go through the motions" at this school.
32. There is a tendency for the superficial to be more important than the substantial at this school.
33. There is a dark tension that exists among key individuals at this school.
34. It seems that the attainment of short-term goals is preferred to the achievement of long-term goals.
35. There seems to be a loss of grace, style, and civility at this institution.
36. There is a tendency to do the minimal and not "go the extra yard" at this school.
37. The administration seems to use coercion to motivate employees here.
38. We do not ever seem to be able to find the time to celebrate accomplishments here.
39. The teachers and staff seem to treat students like customers or impositions here.
40. The employees feel manipulated and exploited here.
41. There don't seem to be many stories and storytellers to carry on the tradition at this school.
42. The leaders here seem to want to be served rather than to serve.
43. There seems to be a certain arrogance among the leaders at this school.
44. There seems to be a sense of competition here whereby one person or group's gain always has to be at another's expense.
45. Teachers here won't pick up a piece of paper because "that's the janitor's job."
46. When something goes wrong here, there is a tendency to want to cast blame.
47. Diversity and individual charisma are not respected here.
48. Teachers here seem to use up all their sick days even if they are not sick.
49. The administration seems to accumulate power rather than sharing it at this institution.

50. The climate in this school seems to encourage competition rather than collaboration.
51. Teachers seem to work solely for a paycheck here.
52. Teachers are asked to teach to the test to improve test scores at this school.
53. There is a tendency for the faculty rooms to be sources of malicious gossip and rumors.
54. There is a union mentality here whereby teachers do not want to do anything extra unless they are paid.
55. Administrators here seem to dwell on people's weaknesses rather than their strengths.
56. Individual turf is protected to the detriment of institutional goals at this school.
57. There is definitely a caste system here among the administration, the faculty, and the clerical and custodian staffs.

THE HEART SMART ORGANIZATIONAL DIAGNOSIS QUESTIONNAIRES

Just as there are vital signs in measuring individual health, we believe that there are vital signs in measuring the good health of organizations. These surveys will help us to identify those vital signs in your school or school system. The purpose of the Heart Smart Organizational Diagnosis Questionnaires, therefore, is to provide feedback data for intensive diagnostic efforts. Use of the questionnaire, either by itself or in conjunction with other information-collecting techniques such as systematic observation or interviewing, will provide the data needed for identifying strengths and weaknesses in the functioning of an educational institution, and help determine whether the leaders are leading with both mind and heart.

A meaningful diagnostic effort must be based on a theory or model of organizational development. This makes action research possible as it facilitates problem identification, which is essential to determining the proper functioning of an organization. The model suggested here establishes a systematic approach for analyzing relationships among the variables that influence how an organization is managed. The Heart Smart Survey II

APPENDIX: DIAGNOSTICS

provides for assessment of three areas of formal and informal activity: moral integrity, a sense of community, and a dedication to service and social justice. The Heart Smart Survey I provides for assessment in ten areas of formal and informal activity (see diagram below). The outer circle in the following table represents an organizational boundary for diagnosis. This boundary demarcates the functioning of the internal and external environments. Since the underlying organizational theory upon which this survey is based is an open-systems model, it is essential that influences from both the internal and external environment be considered for the analysis to be complete.

Structure

How is this institution organized?

Conflict Resolution

Is this institution functional or dysfunctional?

Culture

What values and beliefs are important here?

Goal Setting and Planning

Are the goals clear, accepted, and operationalized?

Leadership

How effectively are the boxes kept in balance?

Internal Environment

Power Distribution

Are the faculty and staff empowered?

Motivation

Are the rewards and incentives effective?

Attitude toward Change

Is this institution continually improving?

Communication

Is the message being transmitted clearly?

Decision Making

How and by whom are decisions being made?

External Environment

The Heart Smart Wheel

APPENDIX: DIAGNOSTICS

HEART SMART SCORING SHEET I

Instructions: Transfer the numbers you circled on the questionnaire to the blanks below. Add each column and divide each sum by seven. This will give you comparable scores for each of the ten areas.

Structure	*Culture*	*Leadership*	*Motivation*
1____	2____	3____	4____
11____	12____	13____	14____
21____	22____	23____	24____
31____	32____	33____	34____
41____	42____	43____	44____
51____	52____	53____	54____
61____	62____	63____	64____

Total
____ ____ ____ ____

Average
____ ____ ____ ____

Communication	*Decision Making*	*Conflict Resolution*	*Goal Setting/ Planning*
5____	6____	7____	8____
15____	16____	17____	18____
25____	26____	27____	28____
35____	36____	37____	38____
45____	46____	47____	48____
55____	56____	57____	58____
65____	66____	67____	68____

Total
____ ____ ____ ____

Average
____ ____ ____ ____

APPENDIX: DIAGNOSTICS

Power Distribution
9_____
19_____
29_____
39_____
49_____
59_____
69_____
Total

_____

Average

_____

Attitude toward Change
10_____
20_____
30_____
40_____
50_____
60_____
70_____

_____

_____

Interpretation Sheet (Heart Smart I)

Instructions: Transfer your average scores from the Scoring Sheet to the appropriate boxes in the figure below. Then study the background information and interpretation suggestions that follow.

Background

The Heart Smart Organizational Diagnosis Questionnaire is a survey-feedback instrument designed to collect data on organizational functioning. It measures the perceptions of persons in an organization to determine areas of activity that would benefit from an organizational development effort. It can be used as the sole data-collection technique or in conjunction with other techniques (interview, observation, etc.). The instrument and the model reflect a systematic approach for analyzing relationships among variables that influence how an organization is managed. Using the Heart Smart Organizational Diagnosis Questionnaire is the first step in determining appropriate interventions for organizational change efforts.

Interpretation and Diagnosis

A crucial consideration is the diagnosis based upon data interpretation. The simplest diagnosis would be to assess the amount of variance for each of the ten variables in relation to a score of 4, which is the neutral point. Scores *above* 4 would indicate a *problem* with organizational functioning.

The closer the score is to 7, the more severe the problem would be. Scores *below* 4 indicate the *lack of a problem*, with a score of 1 indicating optimum functioning.

Another diagnostic approach follows the same guidelines of assessment in relation to the neutral point (score) of 4. The score of each of the seventy items on the questionnaire can be reviewed to produce more exacting information on problematic areas. Thus, diagnosis would be more precise. For example, let us suppose that the average score on item number 8 is 6.4. This would indicate not only a problem in organizational purpose or goal setting, but also a more specific problem in that there is a gap between organizational and individual goals. This more precise diagnostic effort is likely to lead to a more appropriate intervention in the organization than the generalized diagnostic approach described in the preceding paragraph.

Appropriate diagnosis must address the relationships between the boxes to determine the interconnectedness of problems. For example, if there is a problem with *communication,* could it be that the organizational *structure* does not foster effective communication? This might be the case if the average score on item 25 was well below 4 (2.5 or lower) and all the items on organizational *structure* (1, 11, 21, 31, 41, 51, 61) averaged above 5.5.

HEART SMART SCORING SHEET II

Instructions: Transfer the numbers you circled on the questionnaire to the blanks below. Add each column and divide each sum by 19. This will give you comparable scores for each of the three areas.

Moral	*Integrity*	*Community Service/ Social Justice*
1____	2____	3____
4____	5____	6____
7____	8____	9____
10____	11____	12____
13____	14____	15____
16____	17____	18____
19____	20____	21____
22____	23____	24____
25____	26____	27____

APPENDIX: DIAGNOSTICS

28_____	29_____	30_____
31_____	32_____	33_____
34_____	35_____	36_____
37_____	38_____	39_____
40_____	41_____	42_____
43_____	44_____	45_____
46_____	47_____	48_____
49_____	50_____	51_____
52_____	53_____	54_____
55_____	56_____	57_____

Total
_____

Average (Divide by 19)   _____   _____
_____

Average (Divide by 3)   _____   _____
_____

Interpretation Sheet (Heart Smart II)

Instructions: Study the background information and interpretation suggestions that follow.

Background

The Heart Smart Organizational Diagnosis Questionnaires are survey-feedback instruments designed to collect data on organizational functioning. They measure the perceptions of persons in an organization to determine areas of activity that would benefit from an organizational development effort. It can be used as the sole data-collection technique or in conjunction with other techniques (interview, observation, and so forth). The instrument and the model reflect a systematic approach for analyzing relationships among variables that influence how an organization is managed. Using the Heart Smart Organizational Diagnosis Questionnaires is the first step in determining appropriate interventions for organizational change efforts.

Interpretation and Diagnosis

A crucial consideration is the diagnosis based upon data interpretation. The simplest diagnosis would be to assess the amount of variance for each of the three variables in relation to a score of 4, which is the neutral point. Scores below 4 would indicate a problem with organizational functioning. The closer the score is to 1, the more severe the problem would be. Scores below 4 indicate the lack of a problem, with a score of 7 indicating optimum functioning.

Another diagnostic approach follows the same guidelines of assessment in relation to the neutral point (score) of 4. The score of each of the fifty-seven items on the questionnaire can be reviewed to produce more exacting information on problematic areas. Thus, diagnosis would be more precise. For example, let us suppose that the average score on item number 8 is 2.4. This would indicate not only a problem in the sense of community in the institution, but also a more specific problem in that there are not enough occasions provided for the teachers to interact with one another. This more precise diagnostic effort is likely to lead to a more appropriate intervention in the organization than the generalized diagnostic approach described in the preceding paragraph.

REFERENCES

Adams, J. L. 1986. *The Care and Feeding of Ideas: A Guide to Encouraging Creativity*. Reading, MA: Addison-Wesley.
Baker, W., and M. O'Malley. 2008. *Leading with Kindness*. New York: AMACOM.
Bandura, A. 1978. *Social Learning Theory*. Englewood Cliffs, NJ: Prentice-Hall.
Blanchard, K., and S. Johnson. 1982. *One Minute Manager*. New York: William Morrow & Company.
Bolman, L. G., and T. E. Deal. 1991. *Reframing Organizations: Artistry, Choice, and Leadership*. San Francisco: Jossey-Bass.
Brodsky, S. L. 1988. *The Psychology of Adjustment and Well-being*. New York: Holt, Rinehart and Winston.
Carlson, R. 1990. "Conscious Mental Episodes and Skill Acquisition." *Behavioral and Brain Sciences* 13: 599.
Chapple, C. 1993. *The Jesuit Tradition in Education and Missions*. Scranton, PA: University of Scranton Press.
De Pree, M. 1989. *Leadership Is an Art*. New York: Dell Publishing.
Delbecq, A., A. Van de Ven, and D. Gustafson. 1975. *Group Techniques for Program Planning*. Glenview, IL: Scott, Foresman.
Deming, W. E. 2000. *Out of Crisis*. Boston: MIT Press.
Fisher, R., and S. Brown. 1988. *Getting Together*. Boston: Houghton-Mifflin.
Fisher, R., and W. Ury. 1981. *Getting to Yes: Negotiating without Giving In*. Boston: Houghton Mifflin.

REFERENCES

Glasser, W. 1984. *Control Theory, a New Explanation of How We Control Our Lives.* New York: Harper & Row.

Goldaber, I. 1984. *The Communication Laboratory: A Collaboration between Adversaries to Generate Social Change.* Pittsburgh: Pittsburgh Tri-State Area School Study Council, University of Pittsburgh.

———. 1987. *The Goldaber Win/Win Contract Development: A Thirty Day Process.* Miami, FL: Center for the Practice of Conflict Management.

Gordon, J. R. 1993. *A Diagnostic Approach to Organizational Behavior.* Allyn and Bacon.

Greenleaf, R. K. 2008. *The Servant as Leader.* Terre Haute, IN: The Greenleaf Center for Servant Leadership.

Greenwald, A. and Banaji, M. 1989. "The Self as a Memory System: Powerful, but Ordinary," *Journal of Personality and Social Psychology* 57, 41-54.

Hanson, E. M. 1991. *Educational Administration and Organizational Behavior.* Boston: Allyn and Bacon.

Hart, A. W. 1987. "A Career Ladder's Effect on Teacher Career and Work Attitudes." *American Educational Research Journal* 24, no. 4: 479-503.

Heilman, M. E., and M. H. Stopeck. 1985. "Being Attractive, Advantage or Disadvantage? Performance Evaluations and Recommended Personnel Actions as a Function of Appearance, Sex, and Job Type." *Organizational Behavior and Human Decision Processes* 35: 202-215.

Hersey, P., and K. H. Blanchard. 1969. "Life-cycle Theory of Leadership." *Training and Development Journal* 23: 26-34.

———. 1988. *Management of Organizational Behavior.* 5th ed. Englewood Cliffs, NJ: Prentice Hall.

Huber, G. P. 1980. *Managerial Decision Making.* Glenview, IL: Scott, Foresman.

Jones, T. M. 1991. "Ethical Decision Making by Individuals in Organizations: An Issue-Contingent Model." *Academy of Management Review* 16, no. 2: 366-395.

Kaplan, A. 1964. *Power in Perspective.* In *Power and Conflict in Organizations.* Edited by R. L. Kahn and E. Boulding. London: Tavistock.

Kelley, H. H. 1967. "Attribution Theory in Social Psychology." *Nebraska Symposium on Motivation* 14: 192-241.

Kirkpatrick, S. A., and Locke, E. A. 1991. "Leadership: Do Traits Matter?" *Academy of Management Executive* 5, no. 2: 49.

Kotter, J. P. 1977. "Power, Dependence, and Effective Management." *Harvard Business Review* 55: 125-136.

———. 1978. "Power, Success, and Organizational Effectiveness." *Organizational Dynamics* 6: 27-40.

REFERENCES

Latham, G. P., and G. A. Yukl. 1975. "A Review of Research on the Application of Goal Setting in Organizations." *Academy of Management Journal* 18: 824–845.

Lax, D. A., and J. K. Sebenius. 1986. *The Manager as Negotiator*. New York: Free Press.

Lewin, K. 1951. *Field Theory in Social Sciences*. New York: Harper and Row.

Lewis, P. V. 1987. *Organizational Communication: The Essence of Effective Management*, 3rd ed. New York: Wiley.

Lowney, C. 2003. *Heroic Leadership*. Chicago: Loyola Press.

Loyola, I. 2007. *The Spiritual Exercises of St. Ignatius of Loyola*. New York: Cosimo Classics.

Maslow, A. H. 1987. *Motivation and Personality*, 3rd ed. New York: Harper & Row.

Michaelsen, L. K., W. E. Watson, and R. H. Black. 1989. "A Realistic Test of Individual vs. Group Consensus Decision Making." *Journal of Applied Psychology* 74, no. 5: 834–839.

Palestini, R. 2000. *Ten Steps to Educational Reform: Making Change Happen*. Lanham, MD: Rowman & Littlefield Education.

———. 2004. *Ten Steps to Educational Reform: Making Change Happen*, Maryland: Rowman & Littlefield Education.

———. 2011. *Educational Administration: Leading with Mind and Heart*, 3rd ed. Lanham, MD: Rowman & Littlefield Education.

Pavlov, I. 1927. "Conditioned Reflexes: An Investigation of the Physiological Activity of the Cerebral Cortex." Translated and edited by G. V. Anrep. London: Oxford University Press.

Peters, T., and R. Waterman. 1988. *In Search of Excellence*. New York: Grand Central Publishing.

Rahim, M. A. 1989. "Relationships of Leader Power to Compliance and Satisfaction with Supervision: Evidence from a National Sample of Managers." *Journal of Management* 15, no. 4: 545–556.

Ravier, A. 1987. *Ignatius of Loyola and the Founding of the Society of Jesus*. San Francisco: Ignatius Press.

Rest, J. R. 1986. *Moral Development: Advances in Research and Theory*. New York: Praeger.

Senge, P. M. 1990. *The Fifth Dimension: The Art of Practice of the Learning Organization*. New York: Doubleday.

Simon, H. A. 1960. *The New Science of Management Decision*. New York: Harper.

Skinner, B. F. *The Behavior of Organisms: An Experimental Approach*. 1938. New York: Appleton-Century.

REFERENCES

Solzhenitsyn, A. 1978. *A World Split Apart*. New York: Harper & Row.

Thomas, J. B., R. R. McDaniel, Jr., and M. J. Dooris. 1989. "Strategic Issue Analysis: NGT + Decision Analysis for Resolving Strategic Issues." *Journal of Applied Behavioral Sciences* 25, no. 2: 189–200.

Thorndike, E. L. 1924. *Behaviorism*. New York: Norton.

Tolman, E. C. 1932. *Purposive Behavior in Animals and Men*. New York: Appleton-Century-Crofts.

Toner, J. J. 1991. *Discerning God's Will: Ignatius of Loyola's Teaching on Christian Decision Making*. St. Louis, MO: Institute of Jesuit Sources.

Tripole, M. R. 1994. *Faith beyond Justice*. St. Louis, MO: Institute of Jesuit Sources.

Vance, R., and A. Colella. 1990. "Effects of Two Types of Feedback on Goal Acceptance and Personal Goals." *Journal of Applied Psychology* 75: 68–76.

Vroom, V. H., and P. W. Yetton. 1973. *Leadership and Decision Making*. Pittsburgh, PA: University of Pittsburgh Press.

Weber, M. 1947. *The Theory of Social and Economic Organization*. Glencoe, IL: Free Press.

Zuker, R. E. 1983. *Mastering Assertiveness Skills*. New York: AMACOM.

ABOUT THE AUTHOR

Robert Palestini is graduate dean and professor emeritus of educational leadership at Saint Joseph's University in Philadelphia. He is also the founding executive director of the Educational Leadership Institute at SJU. In almost fifty years in education, he has served as a teacher, principal, and superintendent of schools of one of the largest school systems in the United States. He has written more than a dozen books on various aspects of educational leadership.

www.ingramcontent.com/pod-product-compliance
Lightning Source LLC
Chambersburg PA
CBHW070942040526
R18240200001BA/R182402PG44116CBX00016BA/3